TRUE HUMILITY
Finding Power and Joy in This Biblically Mandated Virtue
(revised)

By Norman H. Drummond

Columbus, Georgia

Copyright © 2022 by **Norman H. Drummond**

All rights reserved. No part of this publication may be reproduced, distributed or transmitted in any form or by any means, without prior written permission.

Unless otherwise indicated, Scripture quotations are from the NEW AMERICAN STANDARD BIBLE®, Copyright © 1960, 1962, 1963, 1968, 1971, 1972, 1973, 1975, 1977, 1995 by The Lockman Foundation. Used by permission.

True Humility: Finding Power and Joy in This Biblically Mandated Virtue / Norman H. Drummond -- 2nd ed.

ISBN 978-8-218-10002-5

Dedicated to Mom and Dad

-from whom I caught my first glimpse of how humility looks

CONTENTS

CHAPTER ONE
    DEFINING HUMILITY 1
CHAPTER TWO
    INSIDIOUS PRIDE 21
CHAPTER THREE
    HUMILITY IN THE FLESH 43
CHAPTER FOUR
    HUMILITY ON THE MOUNT 58
CHAPTER FIVE
    JUDGE OR JOY 78
CHAPTER SIX
    HUMBLE BIBLE PEOPLE 93
CHAPTER SEVEN
    LET'S GET READY TO HUMBLE 113
CHAPTER EIGHT
    CHOOSING HUMILITY 140
CHAPTER NINE
    OUR HUMBLE GOD 163
CHAPTER TEN
    EXERCISES IN HUMILITY 176
HUMILITY IN THE PHASES OF MY LIFE 204
ABOUT THE AUTHOR 219
BIBLIOGRAPHY 221

CHAPTER ONE

DEFINING HUMILITY

*"Let nothing be done through selfish ambition or conceit,
but in lowliness of mind let each esteem others better than himself."*
Philippians 2:3

☙❧

Humility: It is attire that many people have never worn or cared to wear. It is probably on our list of least desirable virtues along with generosity, contentment, and whatever the opposite of gluttony is. True Humility? Should we care to know about it? Caring about humility may be like caring about how straight your turned-up pinky is when sipping your tea. We don't really care. Wanting to learn about humility for the purpose of possibly practicing it is like wanting to learn how to become a hermit. It is not on our agenda. Most of us have had feelings of deep desire for fame, fortune, power or a pony. But humility? It may be the single virtue for which we have never felt a hint of yen or pang of desire. We simply do not get excited about being humble. I would love to change that about us.

A Virtue to Hear

It is a peculiar virtue. Maybe humility isn't so odd, but rather we are peculiar when we are confronted by the subject of it.

Consider this quote. "Humility is a virtue all preach, none practice; and yet everybody is content to hear."[1] Those words were penned by John Selden, a 17th century English writer and scholar. His words "content to hear" suggest that we don't mind listening to lessons or lectures about humility. Hearing about it is okay. Lectures, however, will not move us toward the practice of it. There are many good virtues that cause us to flinch upon hearing the pastor announce them as the topic of today's sermon, like: fidelity, generosity, charity, chastity, morality, modesty and more. But humility is a virtue about which we enjoy hearing without being negatively stirred. It's kind of like having positive feelings for preachers with no desire to ever be one. It's like taking delight in the view of a snowcapped mountain without wanting to strap on hiking boots and climb it.

Humility is a good and admirable quality. We are content to hear sermons about it and watch the practice of it by others we admire. But we can't dance to that tune. We choose a different dance to a tune which has rolled around in our heads all week and cannot be drowned out by a tune we seldom hear and to which we have seldom seen others dance. We are content with our lack of humility. Tell us more about humility; we love the stories. Don't, however, expect that we will ever be a humble person.

What Is Humility?

A clear definition of humility may help us reconsider our personal interest in it. A complete and illuminating definition of humility begins with describing what a humble person looks

---

[1] John Selden, *Table Talk: Being the Discourses of John Selden, Esq. . . Relating Especially to Religion and State*

like. Your own description of a humble person may reveal why being humble is not for you. Some people would describe him or her as simple in appearance, bland-colored clothing, head bowed, shoulders forward, shy and unnoticeable. When spoken to, her voice is soft and uncertain. She has few aspirations and low energy. He lacks passion and wouldn't hurt a fly. He is usually alone, and no one wants to emulate his poor, unlovely, pathetic life of humility. What we have just described is a humble demeanor and not humility.

It is no wonder we are uninterested in pursuing humble living if we confuse humble demeanor with meaning to be humble. Learning the difference can change how we think about this powerful virtue. A humble person is quietly confident; neither boisterous, nor woeful. He or she is driven to achieve that which will benefit the Kingdom of God. Her passion is pure and free from selfish intent. He takes delight in the people around him. Her joy or sorrow reflects her compassion and concern for others. If the humble person goes unnoticed, it is because he is continually directing attention away from himself. Her inner strength is enormous, and she does not need praise or credit to feel valued. He is excited about being a part of the world, not the center of it. This is the humble person. He or she chooses a path of lowliness, not listlessness; of meekness, not meaninglessness; of gentleness, not gutlessness. This person is unpretentious, not unambitious; reverent, not irrelevant.

Don't be dissuaded by what is found in a dictionary or thesaurus about humility. Study the Biblical models that represent for us the humble life like Noah, Naomi, Samuel, Esther, Daniel, Mary, John, Tabitha, Barnabas, the mother of Timothy, and Jesus our Lord. These are men and women from whom we can learn humility. These are men and women who can provide us a proper picture of how a humble person looks.

A Scripture-Based Definition

We need a better definition of humility than the dictionary provides. "Not proud" does not define humility nearly enough. How about this? Humility is an active approach to life involving the intentional choice of God and others above self, a determined avoidance of arrogance and pride, and the valuing of service and love far above power, prestige, or personal welfare. Before we can declare this a good and acceptable definition, we need scriptural support. Included in our definition are three aspects of humility: 1. *Do nothing from selfishness or empty conceit, but with humility of mind regard one another as more important than yourselves* (Philippians 2:3); 2. *God is opposed to the proud, but gives grace to the humble* (James 4:6); and 3. *For you were called to freedom, brethren; only do not turn your freedom into an opportunity for the flesh, but through love serve one another* (Galatians 5:13). Humility may involve more but these three basic elements are essential to the kind of humility that God expects of us whenever The Word of God says, *"Humble yourselves"* (e.g., 1 Peter 5:6 and James 4:10). When we seek to be *humble,* we are choosing God and others over ourselves, resisting pride, and giving attention to service and love. Service to God with love for Him and our neighbor will supersede any desire for power, importance, and self-gain that is motivated by sinful pride. This does not mean the humble person will not achieve power, importance, or personal gain. It means that those things are not goals for the humble one, and they are gained in the spirit of humility.

Chapter twelve of Paul's Roman letter is an excellent characterization of humble living. This chapter begins with a call to sacrificial living and to a transformed mind that does not think more highly of ourselves than we ought. That is humility. A quick study of the passage reveals a Christian attitude toward God and others that is humble and not prideful. Allow me to paraphrase, simplify, epitomize and summarize each of these twenty-one verses.

Romans 12
1. Live as is acceptable to God. (12:1)
2. Let God radically transform our minds. (12:2)
3. Be honest in self-appraisal with sound thinking. (12:3)
4. Do not compare your Spirit gifts with those of others. (12:4)
5. We belong to Jesus and need fellow believers. (12:5)
6. Do what God has gifted us to do. (12:6)
7. Preach, serve, or teach as our faith allows. (12:5-7)
8. Be diligent, merciful, liberal, and cheerful in our doing. (12:8)
9. Grab hold of good and hate evil. (12:9)
10. Love like a brother. (12:10)
11. Serve Jesus with passion. (12:11)
12. Let hope be our joy, outlast trouble, and keep praying. (12:12)
13. Take care of Christian brothers and sisters. (12:13)
14. Offer only blessings when others hurt us. (12:14)
15. Be there for others when they are happy or sad. (12:15)
16. Choose lowliness over conceit. (12:16)
17. Choose to respect rather than get revenge. (12:17)
18. Choose peace. (12:18)
19. Let God punish our enemies. (12:19)
20. Provide for the needs of enemies. (12:20)
21. Overpower evil with good. (12:21)

A Sweet Aroma

Humility is a condiment, not the main course. It is a seasoning, not a side dish. Like ketchup on a hotdog, salsa on a taco, or Tabasco on anything, humility makes all Christian action and Christian service better than they are without it. Micah 6:8 says, *"And what does the Lord require of you but to do justice, to love kindness, and to walk humbly with your God?"* Humility does not stand alone; it makes complete the doing of justice and practice of kindness. It is the finishing touch, the rich wood stain on the newly carved altar. Paul described his ministry in Ephesus as, *"serving the Lord with all humility and with tears . . ."* (Acts 20:19). He did not spend his time in Asia being humble among the people. He spent his time serving, working, and laboring, sweetened by a good dose of humility. All of Paul's labors were made more palatable by the humility with which they were offered.

Other Christian virtues mix well with humility. Both in Ephesians 4:2 and Colossians 3:12 we are admonished to behave *". . .with humility, gentleness, and patience."* What a wonderfully delightful flavor is created when these three accompany the forgiving, the love, the obedience, the singing with thankfulness, and whatever we do in word or deed that follows in verses 13-17 of Colossians chapter three. Humility is part of a mixture described in the Bible as adorning the life of those with whom God is most pleased. *"But to this one I will look, to him who is humble and contrite of spirit, and who trembles at My word"* (Isaiah 66:2). Though the word humility is not used in the beatitudes of Matthew 5, we can smell the presence of it in each on them. We see the biblical mandate of humility for Christians and recognize it even when it is not mentioned. Jesus tells us that we "are the salt of the earth" (Matthew 5:13). Humility is an ingredient in that seasoning. Remove humility from that salt, and it has already begun to lose its savor.

Christian behavior encompasses so much more than mere humility. It is not the intention of this book to lift up humility as the only goal or even as one of the greatest goals of the Christian life, but to present humility as essential and indispensable to Christian character. It adds color to the canvas, some kick to the casserole, and some rhythm to the anthem. The Christian life is made richer and more complete with humility.

Humble as Dirt

Complete this defining phrase *"Humble as . . . ."* As what? We might say "humble as a child." That's a possible answer. Descriptive phrases help us define many things: mad as a wet hen, soft as a baby's bottom, cool as a cucumber, fine as frog's hair. There doesn't seem to be a comparison phrase to describe humility that is as enjoyable as these. Maybe we could use some imagination and coin a new expression. If we made up a phrase using alliteration as in "fit as a fiddle" or "pleased as punch," we could say "humble as a hairnet." A lot of things are compared to animals like "bald as a coot" or "sick as a dog". Could humility be compared to a chipmunk or a chihuahua? If we rhymed like the phrases "loose as a goose" or "drunk as a skunk," we might say "humble as a bumble bee." I suppose if we wanted to allude to the lowly aspect of humility we might say "humble as a worm," or "humble as dirt." None of these attempts are satisfying.

Paul pictures the parts of the body as similar to various spiritual gifts with some parts seeming to illicit more praise than others. Following the lead of this lesson in 1 Corinthians, chapter

12, we could coin the phrase "humble as a bellybutton," or "humble as a big toe." If we were to utilize Bible stories where humility is found, we could create from them phrases like "humble as a foot washing," "as humble as a hole in the roof," or "humble as a six-winged seraphim." We might let a reference like "poor as a church mouse" lead us to ideas like "humble as a nursery worker," or "humble as a preacher's wife." None of these suggestions really do it, do they? We may be stuck with the statement "humble as a child." Perhaps it is fitting that even the common comparison phrase about humility is a humble one.

Screwtape to Wormwood

In *The Screwtape Letters,* C.S. Lewis provides imagined communication from a mature devil named Screwtape to his nephew Wormwood. Through his letters, Screwtape helps Wormwood with advice on how devils keep their human assignments from submitting to God's love and purpose. God is referred to as the enemy by these devils, and the human is referred to as the patient. In letter number fourteen, Screwtape directs Wormwood on what to do now that his patient has become humble. He offers this counsel.

> *"Let him [the patient] think of it [humility], not as self-forgetfulness, but as a certain kind of opinion (namely, a low opinion) of his own talents and character. Some talents I gather, he really has. Fix in his mind the idea that humility consists in trying to believe those talents to be less valuable than he believes them to be. . . . The great thing is to make him value an opinion for some quality other than truth, thus introducing an element of dishonesty*

and make-believe into the heart of what otherwise threatens to become a virtue. By this method thousands of humans have been brought to think that humility means pretty women trying to believe they are ugly and clever men trying to believe they are fools. And since what they are trying to believe may, in some cases, be manifest nonsense, they cannot succeed in believing it, and we have the chance of keeping their minds endlessly revolving on themselves in an effort to achieve the impossible."[2]

This is great illustration of what humility is not. It is not thinking less of self, but rather not thinking too much about self. It is not imagining ourselves to be worthless. We are of great worth. We are *"fearfully and wonderfully made"* (Psalms 139:14). The Bible doesn't teach us to undervalue ourselves. We are taught not to think more highly of ourselves than we ought to think *"but to think so as to have sound judgment"* (Romans 12:3). Paul assures us of our worth. *"Do you not know that your body is a temple of the Holy Spirit who is in you . . ."* (1 Corinthians 6:19). We who are in Christ Jesus have been *"given the manifestation of the Spirit for the common good"* (1 Corinthians 12:7). We are not meant to question our value but to make an honest appraisal of it. There is no need to imagine ourselves to be less than God has created us to be. Denouncing and condemning ourselves is not humility. Satan would love to entangle us in this inward conversation that focuses our attention on ourselves and unravels humility. True humility is found in the character of persons with ability, strength, and self-appreciation, who choose to live the humble life of obedience to God and service to God and man. Humility does not reject the self; it rejects

---

[2] C.S. Lewis, *The Screwtape Letters*. 1961 ed., First Touchstone Edition. (New York: Touchstone, 1996) 59.

the attention to self. Humility does not devalue the self; it seeks to more highly value others. Humility does not attempt to destroy the ego; it chooses to let "me" go (or let go of "me"). Humility does not require a meltdown. We must let our candle burn brightly. Our light shines to give God glory. That's humility.

Humbaloney

False humility, like lugubriousness, is rather ignominious. Daffy Duck[3] would say of the falsely humble, "You're despicable!" Actually, he might say that of anyone trying to use the words *lugubriousness* and *ignominious* in the same sentence. Words like that ought to be spread out. Perhaps, they should be left out. *Lugubrious* is defined as "mournful to an exaggerated degree." For example: Her lugubrious expression raised suspicions that her grief was insincere. The word *ignominious* could be replaced with the word *despicable*. What we are saying then is that both false humility and immoderate mourning are detestable and shameful. True humility and sincere mournfulness are related. Neither can be imitated very well. It is usually obvious to casual observers when someone's humility is humbaloney.

The Beatitudes of Matthew 5 describe the elements which are present when humility and mournfulness are real. With each *"Blessed are they"* Jesus described the kind of persons who are the salt of the earth and the light of the world. He was describing His own character and the character of those who would be His disciples. He and they are poor in spirit, . . . mournful, . . . gentle, . . . thirsty for righteousness, . . . merciful, . . . pure in heart, .

---

[3] A Warner Brothers cartoon character that first appeared in the late 1930s as a friend and rival to Bugs Bunny.

.. and peacemakers. Humility contains all these elements. Upon these are the meditations of humble people. Those who epitomize these elements are the ones who are the salt of the earth and the light of the world. Why? They are people who do what the Lord requires, *"to do justice, to love kindness, and to walk humbly with God"* (Micah 6:8). The Beatitudes provide us with great insight into the meaning of humility. Time spent studying these words of Christ, and the teachings that follow in His "Sermon on the Mount," will produce a greater understanding of humility than most Christians possess.

Humble Pie

As we study the meaning of humility, it helps to examine what is not humility. Eating *humble pie* is an excellent expression. This figurative plate of humiliation is an instance where a person does not choose humility but has humbleness forced upon her due to some stupid or careless word or deed. She must eat *humble pie* while also swallowing her pride. The term *humble pie* is believed to have its origin in an actual edible. In some parts of England, a pie was made using the *umbles* or inward parts of a deer. The *umbles* were considered a delicacy, although many people thought them only fit for the lower class or people living a very humble existence.[4] If you had to eat *humble pie*, you were probably in no financial position to be proud. The term was fitting as a reference to humiliation and later lost its connection to the tasty pastry. Eating *humble pie* is not the goal of the person seeking to live a humble life.

---

[4] Charles Earle Funk, *Hog On Ice & Other Curious Expressions* (New York, NY: Harper & Row, Publishers, 1985), 47.

Unless humility is an uncoerced choice, it is neither commendable or in obedience to the scriptural command to *"Humble yourself."* Our definition says that humility involves the intentional choice to place God and others above self. True humility is an elective, not an accident. We desire the kind of humility sought after, not the kind we are forced to eat.

Humbled But Not Humble

Have you ever had a humbling moment in which you behaved without humility? We should act humbly, but we more often react in a way that in no way resembles humility. Humbling occasions are those in which our brains shut down just long enough to lock the car with the keys inside, or look at our watch with the same hand holding a drink, or leave our eye glasses in the seat where we are now sitting. Dumb doings are humbling happenings, but our reaction is curiously guided by pride. We know what that means. We act surprised and amazed that we would be capable of such a silly stunt. "Well! I never!" We look for reasons, blame, or excuses for how it could happen and only after thorough palliation do we begin to own the brain burp with some humility. Humility should be our first response, but most often isn't.

There are times when we find ourselves eclipsed by a person or personality in the presence of someone in whose eyes we loomed large but now not so. We hoped that to this someone we would appear intelligent, powerful, good looking, or sophisticated, but someone else enters the scene who completely outshines us. Faced with minimizing moments, we resist the temptation to be humble and choose humiliation. Ignoring the obvious subjugation, we run at the big dog like the small puppy that thinks he is just as big. Ironically, a humble reaction would probably make us appear much more intelligent, powerful, good looking and sophisticated than that foolish, prideful yipping. Only when we finally embrace humble living, do those humbling moments become opportunities. They are opportunities to say, "It's okay. I choose to be humble." When we are humble, humility doesn't scare us. We recognize a humbling moment as a moment to shine. We choose to be humble, to live humbly, and to face all those humbling times with prior commitment to humility.

Submission And Humility

When we choose humility, we also choose submission. God and others above self, along with service to God and others, is a choice to regard the needs and wishes of God and others as more important than our own. We gladly submit to their will and change our own will accordingly. If this happens by coercion, it is not humility.

A short video of Oprah Winfrey was shown on TV one day during a Hollywood news show. She was crashing a wedding reception, during which she made a toast to the newlyweds. Oprah ended the toast by saying, "and may God hold you in the palm of His hand, but not too tight." Yikes! That is just wrong on a couple of levels. Our temporal and eternal security is found in taking the hand of God. We want Him to hold on tightly. Scripture assures us that nothing can take us out of His hand. Not wanting Him to hold on to us too tightly may be a signal that we are not totally submitted to Him, thus not very humble.

When we are humble before God, we gladly accept His firm grip. Oprah's wish for the newlyweds is a little like saying, "May God keep you secure while allowing you to escape His grip whenever you feel like it, or whenever you want to do something that He may not approve." Submitting to God's authority is humility. We could say submission is humility, but humility is much more than just submission. The two behaviors are inescapably connected to each other. God calls upon us to be humble and obedient. It is a shame to encourage anyone to wish for God to hold them, but not too tightly.

Maybe Oprah thinks our relationship with God is like an earthly one between father and child. The child wants to be able to separate from the Father's authority as the child becomes an adult and establishes independence. It might be acceptable to counsel a parent to hold their children, but not too tightly. We must be willing to allow our children to grow toward independence. Parents have an obligation to give their children wings. Our relationship with God is not the same. God calls upon us to follow Him. He is our great shepherd. Following requires humble submission. We submit to his will and authority all of the days of our lives. Our prayer should be: "Dear God, hold me in your hand, and never let me go. Keep a firm grip upon my life. Don't give me any wiggle room. I want to be in your control always. I humbly choose your complete authority over the purpose and direction of my life."

Pregnant With Humility

As you read these next words, please keep in mind that we are trying to wrap our minds around the meaning of humility. I do not want to offend the reader. I am far too humble to intentionally offend. The example I am about to give is probably a man's twisted perspective. Please accept it as merely another attempt at identifying humility. True humility makes an individual attractive and pleasing, which I think is why an expectant woman is that for me. I have wondered why I am so enchanted with and delighted by the sight of one who is pregnant. It is, I think, because she is so perfectly the picture of humility. She humbly sacrifices her shapeliness, comfort, various vices, foods, and activities, her modesty and her mobility, focusing her total self on the health and well-being on an unseen border, and all of this for nine long pregnant months. No matter how much she may prefer privacy, her transformation into a swollen, bulging, baby basket is a public event. Nora Ephron's protagonist in *Heartburn* said, "There I was, seven months gone, swaybacked, awkward, bloated, logy, with a belly button that looked like a pumpkin stem and feet that felt like old cucumbers. If pregnancy were a book, they would cut the last two chapters."[5] The entire nine months, however, is when the little one teaches the much bigger one great lessons in humility.

It has been told that Marie Antoinette with these words informed King Louis XVI of France that she was pregnant. "I have come, Sire, to complain of one of your subjects who has been so audacious as to kick me in the belly." Punches and kicks from within are generally met with soft words and tummy rubs as mom's humble character adorns her like a gorgeous gown. She is wonderfully beastly. She is grotesquely beautiful. She is dazzlingly disfigured. She is lovely. We enjoy the humility we see in her self-sacrifice to become a conduit through which God will send a new person into the world.

It is a complete lack of humility by which some women choose to terminate their pregnancies, claiming their rights and freedom of choice. Pride and self-centeredness reject the acceptance of responsibility to allow another life to take control of body and future. Thus, the choice to set aside self-interests and

---

[5] Nora Ephron, *Heartburn* (New York: Vintage Books, 1996), 44.

bring about the birth of a child, accentuates the presence of a spirit of humility in the soon-to-be mom. The humble woman submits to the creator who is the giver of all life and, much like the mother of our Lord, she accepts the course that is set with this humble resignation, *"Behold, the bond-slave of the Lord; may it be done to me according to Your word"* (Luke 1:38).

Jesus' mother Mary, and my own mother, and mothers everywhere are, among other things, beautiful examples of submission to the will of God and examples of the nature of humility.

The Unawareness Factor

Humility is a difficult thing to claim. It requires an inattention or obliviousness of it for it to exist. It is somewhat like having guardian angels who watch over us who do not intend to draw our attention to their presence, but only to draw attention to the One who sends them (Hebrews 1:14). We are not meant to worship angels or pray to them. We are to serve God with some awareness that angels are part of God's work to care for us. Neither are we meant to delight in our humility by drawing attention to it. *"Let no one keep defrauding you of your prize by delighting in self-abasement [humility] and the worship of the angels"* (Colossians 2:18).

Perhaps the obliviousness factor is more like what happens when we worship. It is like when we are trying to be true worshippers of God, *"in spirit and truth"* (John 4:24). It is like being vitally involved in a fervent flash of focused attention, emotion, praise and adoration, and we pause in the midst of the experience to tell ourselves, "Now I'm really worshipping!" That abrupt awareness of the *me* in the moment, acts like a belch during a ballad or banana peel at a ballet. When we are walking on stormy seas, the minute we become aware our feet are wet, we lose sight of the Savior, and the miracle ends. It is this way with humility. Mindfulness of humility is no longer humility. We must be humble without picturing ourselves as humble. We must lose ourselves in humbleness and not look back to see if we are there.

No other virtue is quite like humility. For example, we can acknowledge our patient ways and lose none of our patience. We can manifest true love and know that we have loved without spoiling that love. We can be sympathetic and enjoy that truth about ourselves without lessening the degree of our sympathy. Not so with humility. Part of the work of humility is denying self the pleasure of rejoicing in any progress toward it. Maybe very few Christians aspire to know humility because it is something they can never accept a medal for, check-off on their daily planner, or even give God thanks for (e.g., "Thank you Lord for my great capacity at showing humility today in the midst of all those pompous, pride-filled, pew-fillers"). Humility is something we choose to be, because we know it is pleasing to God (Micah 6:8). We concentrate on being humble without wanting a grade for it. We walk humbly without a rear-view mirror. We imitate the humility of Jesus without expecting Him to applaud us. We are humble! We are extremely humble! Ooops! There it went.

Big Enough to Become Little

Vance Havner is a Baptist preacher remembered by many for some great quotables. He was named preacher of the year by the Billy Graham Association in 1973. One of his sayings was, "Too many churches start at eleven o'clock sharp and end at twelve o'clock dull." He also gave us these words: "Few of us are big enough to become little enough to be used of God."[6] Havner wasn't referring to physical size. People of all sizes may behave in big ways or prove to be very small. Our physical largeness or smallness, however, can inhibit humility.

As a short man, it has always been interesting to me how humility can come more easily to a man who is very tall. There are men who, because of their enormous size, have nothing to prove to themselves or others. They are able to take on a meekness and gentleness that is hugely enjoyable, as well as a relief to those much smaller. Some things might be learned from large men about humility that can give us a different twist to the truth in Havner's quote: "Few of us are big enough to become little enough . . ." Small people may act prideful because they have a low perception of themselves, believe others may see them as small persons, and therefore need to display signs of strength for the benefit of themselves and others. They puff up themselves because they are unhappy with being small. Humility doesn't emanate from the lives of those underwhelmed by their smallness. They live under the dark cloud of humiliation.

Actual physical size doesn't have to dictate humility or pride. Humility glimmers from the life of persons who are quietly confident that they are created in the image of God, made sons of God by the blood of Christ, filled with the power of His Holy Spirit, and commissioned to stand against all the forces of evil as a warrior in the Kingdom of God. Because we are wonderfully conscious of who God has made us to be and called us to be, we are able to take on a meekness and gentleness that is hugely enjoyable and far more powerful than any strength that pride might generate. Pride is evidence of smallness. Humility is a pure sign of the presence of power.

---

[6] Dennis J. Hester, comp., *The Vance Havner Quote Book* (Grand Rapids: Baker Book House, 1986).

The Most Humble Man

In Numbers 12:3, Moses is called, *". . . very humble, more than any man who was on the face of the earth."* What a tremendous compliment, especially in light of all that the Bible affords the one who has **true humility**. 1 Peter 5:6 admonishes us, *"Humble yourselves, under the mighty hand of God, that he may exalt you at the proper time."* God certainly exalted Moses, elevating him to the highest position of leadership among God's chosen people and making him the most celebrated person in the history of the Hebrews. Moses' humility made him moldable and usable. It was an act of pride later in the desert which removed Moses from usefulness. The challenge for all of us who want to fulfill God's purposes is to remain humble long after God has exalted us to higher places. This will involve making use of exercises in humility to strengthen our resolve to remain humble before God. Humble people are always aware of the danger of pride and the ease with which we can find ourselves there. This acrostic for the meek is one more attempt at defining humility (although it will not be our last).

- H   honor others (Romans 12:10)
- U   use things, love people (not the other way around) (1 Corinthians 13:1-3)
- M   minimize judgment (Matthew 7:1-5)
- I   inspire others (Acts 3:9-10)
- L   learn from Jesus (Matthew 11:29)
- I   unite with the body of Christ (Colossians 3:12-17)
- T   trust in the Lord (Proverbs 3:5-12)
- Y   yearn for God (Psalm 42 and 63)

Read It Anyway

You can't just say, "Okay, I'm going to be humble." You must picture what that means, live with that perspective, feel it, and know it when it's not there. We will become humble as our desire for it increases. Read a little about humility each day, and you will become more and more conscious of pride and humility. You will become more aware of pride's destructiveness and humility's blessedness. Try it for 30 years, and if you are not satisfied, you can *try* to get your money back. Guaranteed! Have fun with it. Don't make this a chore. For persons who want to live rightly, every day is opportunity to develop character. How great is our desire to be a humble person? Perhaps, not very. My prayer is that God will open our eyes to a new understanding of the value of humility and place in our heart a deep desire to *"HUMBLE YOURSELF."*

CHAPTER TWO

INSIDIOUS PRIDE

> "… and when your herds and your flocks multiply, and your silver and gold multiply, and all that you have multiplies, then your heart will become proud and you will forget the Lord your God …"
> Deuteronomy 8:13-14

The high value of humility in the life of a Christ follower magnifies the extreme danger of pride, the nemesis of humble living. Pride is called *omnium peccatorium mater* - the mother of all sins. Its end is to be feared, and its beginning must be greeted with the same horror. The antidote humility must be swallowed quickly, and then a healthy portion of it smeared on head and heart until all symptoms of pride are erased. Our prayer must be, "Lord if I have not the spiritual strength to choose humility, destroy the pride in me and keep me humble by Thy great power."

At an early stage in the life of the church, leaders felt it was necessary to identify the root causes of moral failures. Their findings were eventually called the seven deadly sins. They determined that all other sins have their beginning in these root sins: pride, greed, envy, wrath, lust, gluttony, and sloth. In "The Parsons Tale" of Chaucer's *Canterbury Tales* the parson explains,

> *"the root of these seven sins is pride, which is the general root of all evils; . . . And though it be true that no man can absolutely tell the number of the twigs and of the evil branches that spring from pride, yet will I show forth an number of them, as you shall understand. There are disobedience, boasting, hypocrisy, scorn, arrogance, impudence, swelling of the heart, insolence, elation, impatience, strife, contumacy, presumption, irreverence, obstinacy, vainglory and many another twig that I cannot declare."*[7]

You may search a good dictionary for an understanding of some of those less commonly used words which Chaucer uses regarding pride. But for now, let us gain a better understanding of *deadly sin*. My definition of *deadly sin* is: One which, by its subtle and seemingly innocent nature, slowly and with little notice stunts spiritual growth, spoils the spiritual fruit, depletes a Christian's spiritual awareness and understanding, and provides the fertile soil for a crop of other more grievous sinful deeds. Of the seven deadly sins, pride is chief. It is a deadly spark that ignites an uncontrollable fire. From it springs a multitude of other sinful attitudes and actions.

Pride is called Satan's sin. It culminated in his attempt to assume the throne of God, followed by God tossing him out on his tail (Revelation 12:9). Pride was the potion that made Satan believe he could conquer the creator. His ultimate end is eternal torment in the lake of fire (Isaiah 14:12-15, 2 Peter 2:4, Revelation 20:10). He, *"The prince of the power of the air, of the spirit that is now working in the sons of disobedience"* (Ephesians 2:2), is a master at luring men to succumb to pride. Pride was

---

[7] Robert Maynard Hutchins, ed., *Great Books of The Western World* (Chicago: Encyclopaedia Britannica, Inc., 1986), vol. 22, *Chaucer*, by Geoffrey Chaucer, 511.

the culprit in the sin of Adam and Eve, when the serpent fed them a lie about the forbidden fruit. His words to Eve were, *"For God knows that in the day you eat from it your eyes will be opened, and you will be like God . . ."* (Genesis 3:5). Man's pride is the infection that lowers his resistance to Satan's attacks. It is the soft underbelly of man that renders him vulnerable to Satan's weaponry. Innocent Eve's story went like this:

TO ADAM'S BRIDE

> The Serpent lied.
> "That fruit you eyed
> Is truth denied."
> "Your eyes," he cried,
> "Will open wide
> No one has died
> Who this fruit tried."
> So Eve complied
> Then testified
> At Adam's side.
> He gratified
> His carnal side,
> Then tried to hide.
> But he God spied
> And clothed with hide,
> Then both were tried,
> Expelled for pride.
> From Paradise,
> Disqualified.
> And all men died.
> Sin multiplied
> Then God supplied
> A lamb who died.

Was crucified.
On Him relied
Those justified,
And glorified,
His chosen bride.
   -By me

I wonder about Adam. The pride that guided his decision to eat the fore-bitten fruit wasn't for the purpose of impressing his beautimous wife. I don't think he was driven by a need to show the animal kingdom he couldn't be pushed around by threats. I don't believe Adam had some self-esteem issue from falling short of his goal to taste every tree in the garden. Adam's temptation had something to do with Satan's offer of godly wisdom. His pride produced a growing confidence that he did not need to consider the consequences of his actions. The man who was commissioned to subdue the earth and rule over every living thing no longer needed to remember limits. After all, the "Tree of the Knowledge of Good and Evil" was one of those living things over which he was ruling. Pride finds its destructive way into the unsuspecting heart. It is a formidable adversary.

A Mature Model

Anything we do well becomes something that pleases us about ourselves and has the potential of developing into sinful pride. Does this mean we shouldn't attempt to do things well? Of course not. It just means we must be diligent about humility and vigilant about pride. Pride surfaces as a judgmental attitude and disdain for those who have not achieved or attempted to achieve what we have achieved. For example, it is a worthy goal to read the Bible through in a year; but that accomplishment is sometimes followed by an ill-opinion of Christians who have yet to do it. An assessment that some Christians are undisciplined and lazy may be true; but when we pat ourselves on the back and others on the head, sinful pride has begun the work of diminishing any spirituality we might have gained. We set a wonderful example for others to follow when we maintain a fervent, persistent, persevering prayer life. All Christians should develop this spiritual discipline. While this is praiseworthy, be aware that pride will impair the appeal and reduce prayer's potency.

Pride obscures many commendable accomplishments and many exemplary qualities. Who hasn't been turned-off by the believer who flaunts her faithful church attendance or brags about his disciplined reading habits, or seeks praise for her lifetime of tithing? Pride always wants us to lift ourselves up and put others down. Even a hint of pride should be shunned. Christians lose the power of their maturity to impact and influence when others perceive that they care more about "look at me" than "follow my model."

Developing spiritually, growing in Christ, becoming more disciplined, fighting the good fight while keeping the faith, and walking worthy of our calling, is the correct path to follow. But, proceed with humility. Maintaining humility as a servant of our Lord must always accompany spirituality. Humility will always make more palatable and desirable our spiritual example, which is the deepest wish of the spiritually maturing disciple of Jesus Christ. We want all Christians to grow to maturity and we care about the value of our example in the process.

Prideful advice is spurned, but humble advice is valued. Consider this scenario. We worked hard and long at a job resulting in both skill and experience. Someone who has neither our skill or our experience walks up and offers advice which is neither solicited nor sensible. Our natural and reflex response is to ignore them, laugh at them, or throw something at them. Humility will look beyond the intrusion and insult to see a person we ought to befriend, encourage, and perhaps even to learn from. Apostle Peter must have bitten his tongue the day Jesus approached his fishing boat. *"Put out into the deep water and let down your nets for a catch,"* said Jesus. There is a little whine in his voice as Peter answers, *"Master, we worked hard all night and caught nothing..."* (Luke 5:5). Fortunately, Peter has a humble moment and continues, *"...but I will do as you say."* In the New Living Translation[8] Peter says, *"But if you say so."*

Pride will invariably cause us to miss God's blessings and miracle moments. If Peter had laughed at the absurdity of Jesus' request and walked away, he would have missed a great revelation of the power of God. Instead, Peter humbly pushed away from the shore, let down his nets, and *"When they had done this, they enclosed a great quantity of fish, and their nets began to break; so they signaled to their partners in the other boat . . . And they came and filled both of the boats, so that they began to sink"* (Matthew 5:6-7). How many moments like this, I wonder, could have been ours had we been living the humble life. Pride pushes God away. Pride preaches "I know what is best for me," and declares "I don't need your direction and interference." Humility submits to God's guidance and heeds His call. What the Scripture says is true. *"Humble yourselves in the presence of the Lord, and He will exalt you"* (1 Peter 5:6). And, we will find that our nets, and our cups, and our lives overflow with God's goodness.

---

[8] Scripture quotations marked (NLT) are taken from the Holy Bible, New Living Translation, copyright 1996. Used by permission of Tyndale House Publishers, Inc., Wheaton, Illinois 60189. All rights reserved.

The Fox and The Crow

Aesop told a story[9] about a crow who, upon finding a piece of meat, flew to a tree holding the meat in her beak. A fox, seeing her and wanting the meat for himself, approached the tree and looking up spoke to the crow, "How beautiful you are, my friend! Your feathers are fairer than the dove's. Is your voice as sweet as you are beautiful? If so, you must be the queen of birds." The crow was so delighted by his praise that she opened her mouth to show how she could sing. Down fell the piece of meat. The fox seized upon it and ran away.

Pride and conceit are easily excited by flattery, even when it is false. When we are focused on ourselves, our ego needs constant feeding, which makes us vulnerable to those who see our weakness. Prideful persons are easily manipulated. Thinking only of themselves, they are unable to see the trap being set or the con being played. A little humility makes us better able to smell baloney and recognize hooey when we hear it. Humility allows us to act according to the life principles to which we are committed. Pride is committed to self. Humility frees us to be committed to a much higher cause. The Christian life is always an impossible one for those who are stuck on themselves. One of the paradoxes of Christianity is that we must lose our life in order to gain it (Matthew 10:39). We must die to self in order to live. We must give ourselves to God in order to become the selves God created us to be. Unless we humble ourselves we will be misled by Satan's flattery and fall captive to his poisonous praise.

---

[9] William J Bennett, ed., *The Book of Virtues* (New York: Simon & Schuster, 1993), 66.

Don't Be a Sorry But

Humility is able to say "I'm sorry." Pride refuses to say the words "I'm sorry" and argues against the need to say it. Most of us find ourselves somewhere in between. We try to fight back the pride so that we can exercise just a little bit of humility. We don't want to be too humble and forfeit all our pride, but we know we probably ought to be, sort of, a little bit humble. When we are about 25% humble and 75% prideful, we are a *sorry, but*. "I'm sorry, but you shouldn't have made me do it." "I'm sorry, but I'm not going to say I'm sorry until you say you are sorry." "I'm sorry, but it really wasn't all my fault." There may be a little humility present in these statements, but pride is still very much in control.

When we are about 50% humble and 50% prideful, we may sound a little like these. "Let's say it together on three, and we will both feel a lot better. Ready, one, two, ..." Or we ask, "If I tell you I'm sorry, will it make you feel better?" At 50/50 our pride is still trying to get something in return for our humility. We will be humble only if our pride is rewarded.

When there is 75% humility present with only 25% pride, we grudgingly say, "I'm sorry. There! I said it! I hope you are happy!" If the apology is accompanied with tears, one wonders if the tears mean they are truly sorry or if they are crying due to the pain of having their pride ripped from their heart. At 75/25, although pride is present, humility is able to produce an apology free from buts or demands. We probably seldom see 100% humility. If a person gets to 75/25, they have risen to a degree of humility most never achieve. To move beyond that requires the strength to set self aside, saving none of the pride, placing oneself in a totally unprotected position, exposing one's feelings to the possibility of attack and accepting the consequences with readiness to take what comes without flinching or fuming or fending.

It may be that the best opportunity for us to discover, learn and develop true humility is when an occasion calls for us to say, "I'm sorry." It is possible that we will find ourselves having the greatest influence or impact upon another life form at a moment when our 83/17 humility blows them away with a sincere and genuine, "I'm sorry." Chances are that at the very moment we achieve the greatest degree of humility we have ever witnessed in ourselves, we will also realize the tenacity of pride as our humble moment quickly fades into delight at how amazingly humble we were. Even still, the struggle to render a humble apology is a worthwhile exercise in humility. And by the way, if this treatise has confused, abused, and failed to amuse, let me say, "I am totally sorry."

The Ass and The Image

One of Aesop's fables is called "The Ass Carrying the Image."[10] Since I am more comfortable with the word *donkey* than the word *ass*, I will tell the story calling the main character *donkey*.

A donkey once carried through the streets of a village a highly regarded wooden image on its way to be placed in a local temple. As the donkey bore his burden, the crowd he passed bowed low before the image. The donkey, believing they bowed their heads out of respect for him, stopped before the crowd, raised his head high with pride, and refused to take another step. His handler, seeing the donkey stop to grandstand, cracked his

---

[10] John R. Long, aesopfables.com

whip between the donkey's shoulders and said, "You obstinate donkey. It has not yet come to this, that men pay homage to a donkey." The moral of the story is: They are not wise who give to themselves the credit due to another. Perhaps another moral to be drawn from this fable is: Our pride is often seen by others as merely a donkey's tail.

Although that may not make much sense, we should recognize in this story one of the traps pride sets for us. Pride tricks us into believing we have reason to be proud. The things about which we want to be proud are almost always things that included the contributions and work of other people. Our self-centeredness only sees our own efforts while others recognize the comparatively small part we played. When we gloat as though we are totally responsible, we merely reveal ourselves to be the ass (or *donkey*) that others know us to be. Pride will always make us look foolish. Humility spares us the shame. Pride is by nature a stumbling stone.

Another of Aesop's fables tells the story of "The Scorpion and the Frog."[11] It seems that a scorpion met a frog, one day, on the bank of a stream. "Carry me across on your back," said the scorpion to the frog. The frog replied, "How do I know you won't sting me?" "Because, if I do," said the scorpion, "I will die too." The frog, pleased with the answer, took the scorpion on his back, set out across the stream, but in midstream the scorpion stung the frog. As paralysis began to take over and cause the frog to sink, just before both would drown he asked, "Why?" Replies the scorpion: "It's my nature." It is the nature of a scorpion to sting. We understand best how to trust any creature when we understand its basic nature. The same is true of pride. Its nature is to destroy. Pride will always drown its lovers. Whenever pride surfaces, we must quickly summon humility to chase it

---

[11] Ibid.

away. The sooner we recognize the danger inherent in pride, the wiser and safer we will be.

King Uzziah

One of the most powerful kings of Judah was King Uzziah. He also had one of the longest reigns as king – 55 years. He was among the kings about whom Scripture says, *"He did right in the sight of the Lord"* (2 Kings 15:3). He was successful against his enemies. He built great cities, and towers, and armies. God made him great. 2 Chronicles 26:8 says, *"and his fame extended to the border of Egypt, for he became very strong."* Unfortunately, the story doesn't stop there. The Chronicler records Uzziah's demise and the reason for it in verse 16. *"But when he became strong, his heart was so proud that he acted corruptly, and he was unfaithful to the Lord his God, for he entered the temple of the Lord to burn incense on the altar of incense."* During a standoff between the temple priests and the king, God struck Uzziah with leprosy. He was made to live in a separate house as a leper, cutoff from the house of the Lord, and was a leper till he died.

"His heart was so proud that he acted corruptly." What a horrible end to the life of one so blessed. Imagine running a masterful marathon and falling flat on your face fifty feet from the finish line. How tragic it would be to climb through the ranks during a stellar thirty-year Army career only to be demoted to Private before retiring. Many mighty warriors in the Lord's army have had a lifetime of service spoiled and rendered ineffective by failing to be on guard against insidious pride.

Proud As Punch

The possible origin of the phrase *proud as punch* underscores the ugliness of pride. *Punch* is the husband in the Punch and Judy puppet show, famous for over 400 years. Though they originated in Naples, Italy about 1600 A.D., Punch is a cultural icon in England. Mr. Punch has a hook nose, hunched back, and flashy costume. The traditional plot of these stringed puppets has Mr. Punch kill his infant child, and then beat his wife Judy to death. After he is thrown into prison, he escapes using a golden key. He then kills a policeman, a doctor, a lawyer, the hangman, death, and the Devil. He murders everyone with huge pleasure, each time repeating his catchphrase, "That's the way to do it!" Punch's pride from outsmarting every figure of authority, according to some, led to the saying *proud as Punch*.[12]

Do not underestimate the ferocity of pride. Punch's fiendish and barbarous behavior is a by-product of pride. Haman, found in the Biblical story of Esther, is an example of the evil outcome of pride. He was elevated to a high position of authority by King Ahasuerus, and soon after, swelled with pride as all the king's servants bowed down and paid homage to him; all except for one man. Mordecai was Queen Esther's cousin who cared for her as a father after his uncle, her father, died. Haman was so outraged at Mordecai's refusal to bow before him that he plotted to have every Hebrew in the kingdom killed. Due to the bravery of the young and beautiful Queen Esther, the plot backfired on Haman, and he was hanged on the very gallows he had built for the purpose of hanging Mordecai.

Pride drives its possessor to commit despicable and dreadful deeds. It is a poison to the soul, a promoter of evil, and the ruin of all that is wholesome and good. We must beware the witchery

---

[12] *Hog On Ice*, 65.

of pride and pray that God will keep our hearts humble. Recognize pride for its true origin and seek humility for its ability to bring us before the throne of God.

Humility and Ambition

The stories of Uzziah and Haman could be taken as lessons against seeking high position. Is ambition equal to pride? Can humility and ambition coexist, or does one eliminate the other? One occasion in the New Testament where ambition was reprimanded was when James and John pressed Jesus for special positions in the Kingdom. Jesus gently refused and later explained to the twelve, *"Whoever wishes to become great among you shall be your servant"* (Mark10:43).

We could interpret this story as a slam against ambition. The instruction, however, has more to do with the focus of our ambition than rejection of it. Our ambition, aim and goals, must become what Jesus wants and not what we have chosen them to be. Jesus gave his disciples a huge goal to achieve. *"Whoever wishes to be first among you shall be slave of all"* (Mark 10:44). Jesus didn't kill their ambition; he redirected it. The command of Jesus in Matthew 28:19 which we call "The Great Commission" is a command to do great things. *"Go therefore and make disciples of all the nations."* There is nothing wrong with ambition as long as it is aimed at achieving the will of God. An attitude of humility allows us to set aside our selfish goals, dreams, expectations, wants and wishes, to fully accept God's ambitious plan and mission. Our love for God results in humble submission. Ambition is connected to pride when it is selfish and rejects God's plan. It has no connection to pride when it is God directed and God receives the glory.

Relationships and Pride

Divorce is not always due to lack of humility, but sometimes is. Jesus ties the act of divorce to the sin of adultery (Matthew 5:31-32). Humility is often the missing ingredient in marriage that could have preserved the relationship if it had been present. What if the husband had been humble enough to admit a mistake, or the wife humble enough to yield to some of his wishes. If she had been humble enough to let him be wrong, or he had been humble enough to do it her way, perhaps love would not have been lost. Humility doesn't have to win. Humility doesn't scream for revenge. Pride stands in the way of reconciliation. It will never give in. Pride will fight for personal victory at any cost. It doesn't care that the resulting divorce is sin. Pride goes before the fall of the once perfect partnership. Humility might have saved it. Pride is the enemy of relationships.

Humility, if turned to in time, can undo damage done by sinful pride. Many men and women will never know a life-long relationship, because they have never known humility. Perhaps they have never known the One who gives eternal life. He is meek and mild. He is the perfect picture of the humble life. And if they know Him, but have never learned humility from Him, then shame on them. They might have had a great relationship with that spouse if they could have been humble like Christ. When pride is in control of either wife or husband, the marriage is at risk.

It isn't only the marriage relationship that suffers because of pride. Pride leads us to pick at every little encounter and conversation. A man misspelled my name in an email and he felt compelled to apologize very quickly. But why? Have we grown so accustomed to the ease with which people get angry that we are gun-shy? Too many today are overly defensive and protective of their image and ego. Those who are incensed when their names are incorrectly pronounced are a bit too full of themselves, too full of pride. Pride is quick to correct and quibble over an inadvertent name garbling. This is one reason pride must be kept in check. When we focus on a small mistake and treat it as if it were a personal attack, we lose sight of the other person. Pride makes us rude, ill-tempered, and easily offended.

If we are unable to control pride-induced wrath when our name is abused, we don't stand a chance at controlling it when someone mounts an ambitious, intentional attack. The struggle to live the humble life is an effort to keep ourselves from flinching when struck by the zings and pings fired by others. Humility's initial reaction is choosing to believe no personal attack was intended. If intentions are discovered to be otherwise, humility seeks to return good for evil and kindness for callousness. Humility is the better way. By humility, room is left for reconciliation. Reacting out of humility prevents the unproductive "tit for tat." Allowing humility to surface instead of pride, protects us from acting in ways which do far more harm to ourselves than to the guilty one. Pride wants to know: does our humble retreat mean that our name is not worth defending? Isn't our name worth fighting to protect? That is our exact point. Pride acts in ways to devalue our name. It is humility that overcomes a need to demand respect for our good name and more effectively preserves it. Perhaps my poem *Downs and Ups* provides further illumination.

DOWNS AND UPS

The proud man will fall.
His conceited life will consist of ups and downs.
Repeated attempts to keep chin up and stand his ground
Will each be met by an inability

To side-step the things that cause stumbling.
His life crumbling, without stability,
He scrambles to pick up the pieces.
Then one day he finds himself singing as his life ceases,
"The record shows, I took the blows, and did it my way."

The humble man will stand.
His lowly life consists of downs and ups,
Prayerful moments on his knees each day erupts
With praise for God's fidelity.
His life humbled more by God's abundant blessings,
Granting him amazing stability
He, the mighty hand of God, increases.
Then one day he finds himself singing as his life ceases,
  "'Tis grace that brought me safe thus far, and grace will lead me home."

Over-Sensitivity/ Under-Humbleness

Over-sensitivity may be a product of very low self-esteem. It is also a product of sinful pride. Pride always carries a big chip on its shoulder waiting for anyone to knock it off. It is quick to take everything people do or say as a personal attack. Pride's need to guard image, appearance, and personal honor results in over-sensitivity. From their book *How to Get Your Husband to Talk to You*, Nancy Cobb and Connie Grigsby provide "a simple test to determine our level of touchiness."[13] They provide us this series of questions.

"Do your feelings get hurt more than once a day?

---

[13] Nancy Cobb and Connie Grigsby. *How To Get Your Husband To Talk To You*. (Sisters, OR: Multnomah Publishers, Inc., 2001) 182-183.

Do you want to 'get even' with people who hurt your feelings?
Do you hold onto grudges longer than a day?
Do you readily accept the apologies of those who offend you?
Do you pout?
Do you withdraw from your 'offender'?
Do you give your offender the silent treatment?
Do you sometimes forget why you got mad in the first place?
Do you let others' treatment of you affect the way you treat them?
Do you withhold forgiveness until the one who hurt you apologizes?
Do little hurts bother you?
Do you become defensive regarding constructive criticism?
Do people have to tread lightly around you?
Do you prefer to think of yourself as a sensitive person?"

Our answers to these questions may expose the presence of pride. The person who is too sensitive will react badly to many harmless situations and innocent comments. Those uncalled-for and unwarranted responses escalate into embarrassment and distress. Hypersensitivity calls the sincere, sinister. It labels the unoffending, offensive. It sees the blameless as dark-hearted. What is difficult to see is the pride at the core of our oversensitivity.

It is of little help to identify a problem without providing a solution. The solution to oversensitivity is good dose of humility. A little humility allows us to more accurately define the actions of others with proper objectivity rather than subjectivity and suspectivity. Humility sets the self aside and examines words and deeds with grace, hope, and love. These three attitudes are missing in the hypersensitive person. When the pain caused by oversensitivity drives us to our knees, we may discover, at the moment of our praying for relief, that God directs us toward recovery and repair on a path called *the humble life*.

It Is Hard to Be Humble . . .

Let's have a little fun. Picture the following, and imagine how easily pride can surface. It is probably just playful, innocent pride. There is probably no harm done by pride in these moments. Or, is there? It is hard to be humble . . .

When looking in a mirror
While holding your grandchild
While holding a taser
While holding four aces
After catching an 8 pound bass
After catching the thief who grabbed your wife's purse
After watching your husband do something stupid
After catching the bouquet
While driving a Corvette
While driving a Zamboni
When riding an elephant
When wearing a custom made, silk, three-piece suit
When wearing an Elvis jumpsuit
When wearing a monocle
After completing an obstacle course
After completing a Rubix Cube
After earning a college degree

In what situations or circumstances do you find it hard to be humble? Though it may be hard to be humble, we should not excuse ourselves from trying. Let me remind us once more – pride is insidious and dangerous.

The Enemy of Peace

Pride is a great spoiler of peace and contentment. I watched a man who was much older than I insist on participating in work from which his age could easily have excused him. Pride drives him, as it does many men and women, to attempt things that are as unnecessary as they are dangerous. A little humility would allow him to avoid injury, enjoy the peace and tranquility of old age, and resist the desire to prove "I can still do it."

Pride does the same to young people. It causes young men to refuse help or advice from their wife or mother. It causes young women to resist assistance from their husband or father. Pride turns a harmless situation into competition. It keeps us on edge and guarded. Humility can un-ruffle feathers, allow the blood pressure to return to normal, and drop the defensive barriers which we so quickly erect. Pride is our enemy. It is the enemy of relationships, progress, and good health. I know of a man who drove the loop around Atlanta for three days because his pride kept him from asking for directions. Actually, I made this up . . . but it could happen.

Pride doesn't keep us from going places, but it keeps us from getting places. I ate at a restaurant once because I was too proud to walk away when I realized I was at the wrong restaurant. I bought an extra item at the hardware store one day because my pride wouldn't let me stand in line at the register with only a fifty-cent item. Pride makes us crazy. Have you ever dangerously pulled away from a side road into oncoming traffic because you were worried what the people in cars waiting behind you might think about you if you took too long? That's pride at work. When God demands that we become humble, it is for our own good. God wants us to drop the pride and enjoy the abundant life. With pride out of the way, we can lean upon God, learn from God, and realize the peace and contentment that He has granted all who love Him and humbly trust in His Son. Proverbs 22:4 says, "The reward of humility and the fear of the Lord are riches, honor and life."

The Insanity and Endless Cycle of Pride

Humility is a better master than pride. Humbleness allows reason and sensibleness to shape our actions and reactions. Pride drives us to behave out of narrow-mindedness and senselessness. Pride offers few choices in tense or precarious situations while humility calmly sorts through available options. President Lincoln is credited with saying, "Better give your path to a dog than be bitten by him in contesting for the right."[14] In many such contests, pride will refuse to give way. Humility is able to see the opponent as merely a dog and take wiser steps. Pride ignores wisdom, while humility side-steps foolish selfishness and selfish foolishness.

A life of pride can expect to be oft bruised. The person who practices a life of humility will be seldom bitten and will be amused by the imprudence of those governed by pride. Proverbs 16:18-19 explains, *"Pride goes before destruction, and a haughty spirit before stumbling. It is better to be humble in spirit with the lowly than to divide the spoil with the proud."* Pride

---

[14] Louise Bachelder, ed., *Abraham Lincoln, Wisdom & Wit* (Mount Vernon, New York: The Peter Pauper Press, 1965) 46.

does not only lead us to fall; pride seems to seek out the stone upon which to trip. The humble life recognizes the dangers of pride and chooses to walk uprightly rather than stumble. A prayer for humility is a prayer to be set free from the insane control of pride and return to the sanity of humility.

Learning to identify indicators of pride is a goal of humility. Poor choices and wrong reactions are always part of life when pride takes charge. When we watch for behaviors that indicate pride and remind ourselves that nothing good can come from them, we can resist the downward pull of pride.

Major indicators of pride are moments that are self-centered ones when the theme becomes *Me*. In those moments we will be tempted to say things like, "It isn't fair", or "It's my turn", or "Why is this happening to me?" These thoughts are followed by "Why do I always get stuck with the dirty work?", or "Why do I have to put up with this?" Feelings like these are usually justified by words like "It is normal for me to feel this way", or "I have a right to feel like this." When we are comfortable with our self-focus, we give ourselves permission to let sinful pride drive us to make a wrong choice and react poorly. Afterward, we feel regret and shame. We apologize and recommit ourselves to humility. For a short while we may be more careful about becoming prideful. Eventually, however, the cycle is likely to be repeated.

If we learn nothing from our mad, mean moments, we will go through that cycle again and again. Humility is always the best disposition and pride always the worst. Pride is a factor in every moment where we act in ways that we will later wish we could erase and undo. And then, there are times when we react humbly and later wish we had been tougher, meaner and more demanding. We imagine a non-humble action might have gained for us something positive and rewarding. That thinking leads us to behave the next time with angry, uncontrollable pride. Then, once again, comes regret and shame. We apologize and recommit ourselves to humility. For a short while we are more careful about becoming prideful. When will the cycle stop?

CHAPTER THREE

HUMILITY IN THE FLESH

"Being found in appearance as a man, He humbled Himself by becoming obedient to the point of death, even death on a cross."
Philippians 2:8

What Jesus did when He left The Father's side to become flesh and dwell among us was a little like a zillionaire choosing to leave his mansion to live in a homeless shelter. Please don't be offended. We are trying to grasp the humility of His leaving Glory. There is nothing on earth that can compare. Anything a human might do, that would remotely resemble what Jesus did, would be tainted by imperfect motive and defective virtue.

Jesus is God the Son. He and the Father and the Spirit are one. It is this Godhead of whom the Psalmist speaks.

"The Lord reigns, He is clothed with majesty; The Lord has clothed and girded Himself with strength; Indeed, the world is firmly established, it will not be moved. Your throne is established from of old; You are from everlasting" (Psalm 93:1-2).

> *"The Lord has established His throne in the heavens, and His sovereignty rules over all" (Psalm 103:19).*

God the Son, in an event impossible for us to fully comprehend, arose from his throne, stepped away from His regal robes, laid down His royal scepter, and bowed Himself to the earth.

In John's gospel just before the betrayal by Judas, Jesus had an intimate moment with the Father. As we read His prayer, we feel as if we are eavesdropping on a private conversation. The prayer is almost too personal for us to hear. The Son reported to the Father the completion of His mission and requested special favor for His followers. In this prayer, we hear His claim of pre-existence and equality with the Father. *"I glorified You on the earth, having accomplished the work which You have given Me to do. Now, Father, glorify Me together with Yourself, with the glory which I had with You before the world was"* (John 17:4-5).

How unselfish! We know that God loves us. But at what price? The cost for Jesus was to leave Glory. That action required an unimaginable sacrifice. *"Although He existed in the form of God, [He] did not regard equality with God a thing to be grasped, but emptied Himself . . . He humbled Himself . . ."* (Philippians 2:6-8). What spiritual contortions were required for the Son of God to empty Himself? Paul simply called it humility.

The Humility of Coming to Earth

If leaving Glory was amazing humility, imagine the self-sacrifice when God subjected Himself to human birth. He went from creating woman, to being born of a woman; from being clothed in glory, to being wrapped in swaddling clothes. God who spoke the world into existence was now saying ga-ga. He moved from omnipresence to limiting Himself in time and space. That is humility!

> *"Joseph also went up from Galilee, from the city of Nazareth, to Judea, to the city of David which is called Bethlehem, because he was of the house and family of David, In order to register along with Mary, who was engaged to him, and was with child. While they were there, the days were completed for her to give birth. And she gave birth to her firstborn son; and she wrapped Him in cloths, and laid Him in a manger, because there was no room for them in the inn." (Luke 2:4-7)*

Imagine the humility of God in this birthday scene. If we were able to imagine ourselves there, we might question the entire arrangement. "Ok, let's be born in the city, a big city. A big important city . . . Bethlehem? Why there? My earthly father is Joseph and my mother is Mary. What? Unmarried? With child? She gave birth to her firstborn? You mean there will be siblings? And . . . I am sleeping in what?"

Please don't mis-understand this. Jesus knew exactly what leaving Glory would involve. His choice of obedience to the Father was made with the full knowledge of the events that would occur. He was not forced into a humbling or humiliating existence. *"He emptied Himself"* (Philippians 2:7). *"He humbled Himself"* (Philippians 2:8). He doffed His royal regalia and donned finite flesh. His entry into our world of pain and impairment was premeditated humility.

Christmas is a very humble season. It is a time to gather our family around us and celebrate the blessings of kinship. We move from celebration to celebration enjoying our children, grandchildren, brothers and sisters, parents and grandparents, uncles and aunts. There is merry laughter. We have warm fireplaces and cold drinks. Life is good, just like the very first Christmas when Mary and Joseph and Jesus . . . and sheep . . . and those persons who didn't have room . . . and maybe some cats, gathered to celebrate a baby's birth. Well perhaps theirs was a little different than ours.

What a humble holiday Christmas is! I love it. I put strings of lights on the house, in the yard, and on the tree. My wife and I drive around the neighborhoods to see lots of houses with red, green, blue, white, and red, and silver lights and stuff. There are light-up reindeer, and wreathes, and Mickey Mouse, and Winnie the Pooh, and light-up manger scenes that remind us of that first Christmas when Mary and Joseph and Jesus had . . . a star . . . and maybe a lamp . . . and a distant light in the window of that inn full of people. Hmmmm!

Perhaps the humble season of Christmas is expressed with gifts. I remember one year getting a toy shotgun with a rabbit that ran on batteries. It was great until the rabbit was left on the floor furnace. Christmases consist of memories of special gifts all wrapped up in beautiful paper and ribbon. Lots and lots of present getting and giving is what makes Christmas special, just like that first Christmas when the Magi brought the baby Jesus some great gifts, even if they were about a year late . . . and just before all of those children were killed. Okay! Our Christmases may not resemble the event of Christ's birth. So what should we do?

Maybe the most humble moment of Christmas is when we set aside the "twas the night before Christmas," pick up the Bible, get quiet and reverent, and stop thinking about ourselves to read aloud verses from Luke chapter two. *"When the angels had gone away from them into heaven, the shepherds began saying to one another, Let us go straight to Bethlehem then, and see this thing that has happened which the Lord has made known to us. So they came in a hurry and found their way to Mary and Joseph, and the baby as He lay in the manger"*(Luke 2:15-16). It is when our eyes become misty upon hearing again the wonderful story of God's great love, and for a brief moment we are unable to see the lights and the gifts and family members next to us, that the humble season of Christmas is filled with real joy, and The Light, and the greatest gift ever.

The Humble Story of His Birth

There doesn't seem to be much about the way we observe Christmas that teaches humility. Our celebration of Christ's birth with an abundance of lights, colorful packages, visions of sugarplums dancing in the heads of good little girls and boys; a rosy-cheeked fat man dressed in fur from his head to his feet; and enough food to choke a horse is not an exercise in humbleness, gratefulness and blessedness. The only glimpses of humility come from the voices of Tiny Tim saying, "God bless us everyone," and little Zuzu saying, "Look, Daddy! Teacher says every time a bell rings, an angel gets his wings."

The scarcity of humility in our celebrations of Christmas is odd. Christmas began with such a different tone and flavor. The birth of Christ was bursting with humility. The Christmas story put the spotlight on a very young virgin who humbly accepted the wishes of her God, a young man who yielded to a path he would not have chosen for himself, a humble stable in a small humble village, a cattle trough baby crib surrounded by simple shepherds, and a small baby boy who nine months earlier had occupied a seat next to His Father in Glory. The midnight scene of a young newlywed couple, far from family, in a land controlled by a brutal foreign government, roughing it in an animal shelter, wondering at this brand new, God-given, surprise responsibility, and wondering about their precarious future, is a picture totally unlike the typical American Christmas. Theirs was a humble night, with only starlight. The only carolers were cows, no family but each other, the only gift a child. The smiles they wore were not placed there by the sight of lavishness, but by the quiet confidence that they were in the center of God's will. The joy that filled their hearts did not arrive by sleigh but by the promise of God. Their evening focus was not on self or each other. The center of their attention was the incarnation of God, God in the flesh. God looked into their eyes from His manger bed reaching up to hold their finger in His hand.

For the parents of Jesus, humility was not an effort but a natural part of the moment. Humility is always the apparel worn by those for whom Christmas is not about getting gifts but about gazing at God's glory. We must take off our garments of gold, nonsense and mirth and put on humility. Only then are our ears able to hear the invitation of Christmas: "O Come, let us adore Him, Christ the Lord!"

The Spirit of Jesus' Birth

What is the spirit of Christmas? What Christian attitude or virtue is most evident during this festive season? What spirit permeates this Bible story? There are three most often heralded: (1) Joy- Luke 2:10, *"Do not be afraid; for behold, I bring you good news of great joy which will be for all the people."* (2) Peace- Luke 2:14, *"Glory to God in the highest, and on earth peace among men."* (3) And love- John 3:16, *"For God so loved the world that He gave His only begotten Son."* These three attitudes are found in all of the Christmas carols, cards, tree ornaments, sermons, and personal greetings. What Christian attitude is least celebrated at Christmas? Humility. Consider this: The Christian attitude which best compliments the Christmas story of joy, peace, and love is humility.

Why not preach a Christmas message on humility? Rather than "Merry Christmas," why not greet each other with, "May your Christmas be humble!" Let's send Christmas cards with wishes for God's Spirit to fill our homes with humility. And, let nothing adorn our home or tree that is materialistic, selfish, vain, immodest, or arrogant. Let our celebration be Christ-centered and our merriment expressed meekly.

Should I Celebrate Christ's Birth?

It has been trendy with Christians today to question the validity of various Christian customs and celebrations. I have heard more than one pastor mention that the Bible never tells us to remember Christ's birth but only to remember His death. This is true. Jesus, at the last supper with his disciples, instituted the eating of bread and drinking of wine "in remembrance" of his body and blood. Paul adds that as Christians share in The Lord's Supper we are proclaiming "the Lord's death until He comes" (1 Corinthians 11:26).

But what about the birth of Christ? The Incarnation? What about the events involved when God the Son came to earth? Does it have no significance that we should celebrate it? We celebrate the special days of those we love, don't we? Why should the birthday of our Lord be any different? For all who believe in Jesus, the virgin birth was a special day. It was the event which fulfilled Prophecy that signaled God's favor and the dawning of a new day. *"For a child will be born to us, a son will be given to us; And the government will rest on His shoulders; and His name will be called Wonderful Counselor, Mighty God, Eternal Father, Prince of Peace"* (Isaiah 9:6). The event of Jesus' birth was so important that Matthew and Luke, under the inspiration of the Holy Spirit, spent two chapters each on the Christmas story. John found it important enough to our doctrinal understanding of who Jesus was to affirm, *"And the Word became flesh, and dwelt among us"* (John 1:14).

The birth of Christ was so important that heaven's angels came to announce it to shepherds in the field, and a star appeared in the sky to direct magi to the event. Why does God make such a celebration of the event if not to indicate to us that it is an event to celebrate? Simeon celebrated the birth of Jesus. This man had been told by the Holy Spirit he would not die until he had seen the Messiah. When Mary and Joseph brought the eight-day-old baby to the temple, Simeon took Jesus into his arms and blessed God. Simeon celebrated this special birthday as did angels, wise men, shepherds, and Scripture.

Jesus died on a cross to complete His work on earth to redeem us from sin. We will always celebrate that sacrifice, which was necessary for our salvation and the greatest expression of God's love. We celebrate His birth because it was that day when the little lamb arrived as a humble child who would live a humble life and die a humble death. Rejoice! The Lord is come! Celebrate! Your Savior is born! God is with us!

The Humility of Living In Earth

From His heavenly throne to a body of flesh, Jesus entered a humble existence among us. The Gospel of John opens with a description of this extraordinarily humble event.

> *"In the beginning was the Word, and the Word was with God, and the Word was God. He was in the beginning with God. All things came into being through Him, and apart from Him nothing came into being that has come into being. In Him was life, and the life was the light of men" (John 1:1-4).*

> *"He was in the world, and the world was made through Him, and the world did not know Him. He came to His own, and those who were His own did not receive Him" (John 1:11).*

The Son of God came to the people of God and was snubbed. Most of the people did not notice that God was walking amongst them. They saw only the son of Joseph. They saw a man with dusty feet, calloused hands, and tanned skin. They could not see beyond His Jewishness that He was not ordinary man. But, His identity did not escape everyone.

> *"And the Word became flesh, and dwelt among us, and we saw His glory, glory as of the only begotten from the Father, full of grace and truth" (John 1:14).*

His manifest humility also did not go unrecognized by everyone. John the Baptizer objected upon being asked by Jesus for baptism. *"I have need to be baptized by You, and do You come to me?"* (Matthew 3:14). John knew himself to be unworthy to even assist Jesus with the menial task of un-strapping His shoes. There was no doubt that he was unworthy to baptize Jesus. John yielded to Christ's request and held humility in his hands. An undeserving crowd watched as John received God's Son into the dirty waters of the Jordan. He lowered the Savior beneath the cool water until He was completely submerged, then assisted Him upward. Before his startled eyes, John watched his conviction confirmed as the Spirit of God descended upon the Savior. John's testimony later was with absolute certainty, *"I myself have seen, and have testified that this is the Son of God"* (John 1:34). God was revealing Himself to us. He is a God with such great love that He would make Himself one of us, one with us, one for us.

His demonstration of humility was followed by instruction that we should be humble also. *"But the greatest among you shall be your servant. Whoever exalts himself shall be humbled; and whoever humbles himself shall be exalted"* (Matthew 23:11).

A Little Place For Me

I wrote most of the poems found in this book. This one, however, is credited to V. Raymond Edman. The poem illustrates for us the constant struggle to be humble.

"Father, where shall I work today?"
And my love flowed warm and free.
Then He pointed me out a tiny spot,

And said, "Tend that for me."
I answered quickly, "Oh, no, not that.
Why, no one would ever see,
No matter how well my work was done.
Not that little place for me!"
And the word He spoke, it was not stern,
He answered me tenderly,
"Ah, little one, search that heart of thine;
Art thou working for them or me?
Nazareth was a little place,
And so was Galilee."

The life of Jesus on earth, although His ministry was brief, was filled with demonstrations of Jesus' power, authority, and humility. For an understanding of what true humility is and looks like, one needs to look no further than the life of Jesus. Every choice of an apostle, every public event, every sick and needy person He encountered, every revelation of Himself is a lesson for us in humility.

The Humility of Dying For Sin

"When they came to the place called The Skull, there they crucified Him and the criminals, one on the right and the other on the left. But Jesus was saying, 'Father, forgive them; for they do not know what they are doing'" (Luke 23:33-34). The cross was one of the most shameful, disgraceful, humiliating, and painful methods of punishment. For Jesus to accept death on a cross was a choice to display the magnitude of His love. His death is not about being pitiful and weak; it is about offering an unselfish, totally selfless, sacrifice.

Humility involves taking a step away from self and toward another. When we are humble that can happen. Pride is self-centered and unable to detach from one's own self-interests. The greater the distance of the step away from self involves increasingly greater amounts of humility. Throwing one's self on a grenade or taking a bullet to save someone reveals a courageous and heroic spirit of humility. Let me qualify that statement. If the acts just mentioned are nothing more than trained or programmed reflexes, then they may not involve humility, courage, or heroism. I would like to believe even hardened professional soldiers do not react from a purely programmed impulse. There must also be courage and humility present for the bravest, most unselfish choices.

Smaller steps away from self are also commendable. Self-sacrifice and humility are necessary to bite your tongue when tempted to attack, to allow someone else to be the center of attention, to absorb unjust criticism, to listen a little longer than we would like, to allow someone else's idea to eclipse our own, to take the blame for someone else's mistake, to applaud something we might rather criticize, to bend instead of stiffen, to smile instead of scowl, to agree when we have every right to disagree, and to choose peace when anyone else in our shoes might start a war.

None of these are easy. In fact, they all demand the strength of true humility. They are all a little bit like taking a bullet or falling on a grenade. You might even say some of these situations feel like being nailed to a cross. Following Christ, taking up our cross daily, involves learning a lot about the humility of Christ. He stepped away from himself to bear our burden. He sacrificed his life, so that we could live. He died, not for His own sins, but for ours. *"He humbled himself by becoming obedient to the point of death, even death on a cross"* (Philippians 2:8). Every step Jesus took, from His throne and back again, demonstrated God's love, mercy, grace, long-suffering, and humility. Paul asks us to pay attention to the attitude of Christ, and emulate that attitude.

> *"Do nothing from selfishness or empty conceit, but with humility of mind, regard one another as more important than yourselves; do not merely look out for your own personal interests, but also for the interest of others. Have this attitude in yourselves which was also in Christ Jesus, who, although He existed in the form of God, did not regard equality with God a thing to be grasped, but emptied Himself, taking the form of a bond-servant, and being made in the likeness of men. Being found in appearance as a man, He humbled Himself by becoming obedient to the point of death, even death on a cross." Philippians 2:3-8*

Let's be clear. God glorified the Son because He humbled Himself and was obedient to the Father's will. He is glorified by the Father, not because He was bruised and suffered a cruel death, but because His death was necessary for our salvation. Jesus' humility is seen, not in His pain, bruising, and sorrow, but in His willingness to become the sacrifice for our sins. He took our punishment for us. It was His punishment that we deserved. *"He was pierced through for our transgressions, He was crushed for our iniquities; the chastening for our well-being fell upon Him, and by His scourging we are healed"* (Isaiah 53:55).

PAY ATTENTION!

Jesus was not born in a prestigious town.
His mother and father were not high society.

He did not enter the world in robes of purple.
He did not carry a jeweled scepter.
He did not come to us in gleaming glory.
He did not burst on to the scenes of history riding a white horse.
He was not escorted by the wealthy or powerful.
He did not achieve, acquire, triumph, or climb the ladder of success.
He had no long life to leave a legacy.
When taken to court, no high-priced lawyers defended Him.
When sentenced, he received no leniency.
His death was not heroic, daring, or noble.

He was born
In a little town called Bethlehem,
To a virgin,
And a carpenter,
In a cave,
Far from family
Surrounded by hay and stars,
He was welcomed by shepherds
and later a few unknown wisemen from an unknown country.
For His first birthday soldiers killed all male babies two years
old and younger.
He grew up as a redneck from Galilee,
His father died before he was 30,
He became an itinerate preacher,
Surrounded himself with fishermen and outcasts,
And was on the public scene only briefly.
Ultimately, His followers deserted Him.
Liars and schemers had him arrested, tried, and convicted.

He was publicly whipped and beaten.
While waiting his execution, he was laughed at and rudely mistreated.
He was forced to carry the instrument of his death through the streets.
He was hung as a criminal on a cross while His mother watched.
Even while dying, he was mocked and tormented.

Humility was evident from the Godhead, to the manger, in Galilee, in His gospel, entering the Golden Gate, in the grape juice, in the Garden, in the synagogue, at Golgotha, and the grave. All that He did was for us, because it was necessary to provide forgiveness of sin to every believer and eternal life to those who call Him King.

CHAPTER FOUR

HUMILITY ON THE MOUNT

*"When Jesus saw the crowds, He went up on the mountain;
and after He sat down, His disciples came to Him, He opened his mouth
and began to teach them, ..."*
Matthew 5:1-2

❧

The word humility appears nowhere in it, yet Jesus' sermon in Matthew chapters five through seven has an abundance of lessons related to humble living. The first twelve verses, called "The Beatitudes," provide a list of evidences of humility. *"Blessed are the poor in spirit . . . those who mourn . . . the gentle . . . those who hunger and thirst for righteousness . . . the merciful . . . the pure in heart . . . the peacemakers . . . [and] those who have been persecuted for the sake of righteousness."*

The definition of humility given in chapter one was this: an active approach to life involving the intentional choice of God and others above self, a determined avoidance of arrogance and pride, and the valuing of service and love far above power, prestige, or personal welfare. Each of "The Beatitudes" are *be attitudes* that involve (1) putting God and others above self, (2) resisting pride, and (3) desiring service and love more than things. The *be attitudes* are found in humble people and lauded by a humble Lord. How closely related to humility are these lessons given in Christ's classic sermon? After our look at each lesson, we can grade the degree of humility necessary to behave as Jesus' commands. On a scale of 1 to 10, ten will represent a high degree while one will indicate a low score of humility.

Peacemakers (Matthew 5:9)

"Blessed are the peacemakers." Peacemakers are humble people. To be one, we must be more interested in peace than in getting our own way. We must be humble enough to swallow pride, let our own desires take a backseat, and let personal passion subside, in order to negotiate a settlement which results in peace. Peacemaking isn't easy. The humility required for this tedious work doesn't come easy either. Peacemakers confront highly explosive situations with a gentle, merciful and pure heart and without fear of persecution. They disarm the aggressor with humility and win the peace. Godly virtue is necessary for peacemaking.

Making peace isn't always possible. When given two persons, or two groups of people who want their way at any cost and will not listen to reason or consider compromise, peace may not be reachable. The humble person attempting to be a peacemaker cannot expect to be successful every time. Humility allows the peacemaker to recognize a stalemate and patiently wait for a future opportunity with better chances for a peaceful outcome. This is the humility our Heavenly Father manifests in his making peace with men.

Jesus began each beatitude with *"blessed are those . . ."* and followed each with their blessing. *"Theirs is the kingdom of heaven . . . they shall be comforted . . . they shall inherit the earth . . . they shall be satisfied . . . they shall receive mercy . . . they shall see God,* and *theirs is the kingdom of heaven."* Of the peacemakers Jesus said, *"They shall be called sons of God."* Perhaps more than any other virtue mentioned, peacemaking more clearly identifies us to the world as ones who behave like the Father.

10 - 9 - 8 - 7 Your Peace Making Humility Score 4 – 3 – 2 – 1

Humility and Persecution (Matthew 5:10-12)

"Blessed are those who have been persecuted for the sake of righteousness." Willingly and joyfully suffering persecution for the cause of Christ is a beautiful demonstration of humility. Pride demands revenge for an offense. It runs from the humiliation of persecution. Humility reacts differently. Blessed are those who with humility will allow persecution without getting defensive, suffer persecution without regret, and receive the persecution without shame. These actions happen only out of an attitude of selflessness. Humility knows that the righteousness for which we are being persecuted is not our own. Ours is as filthy rags. We are persecuted for the sake of the righteousness that we possess in Jesus Christ. We are blessed, Jesus said, when we are persecuted because of Him. We humbly accept persecution knowing Jesus humbly accepted the humiliation of bearing our sin upon a cruel cross.

The stark meekness involved in the persecution of Christ on the cross is prophesied by Isaiah. *"He was oppressed and He was afflicted, yet He did not open His mouth; like a lamb that is led to slaughter, and like a sheep that is silent before its shearers, so He did not open His mouth"* (Isaiah 53:7). Jesus illustrated the strength of humility when facing oppression. Christians can do more than merely endure abuse. We can reflect the character of Christ by receiving persecution with humility.

We must wonder at the powerful image burned into the mind of a young man named Saul when he watched the stoning of Stephen. The crowd kept stoning Stephen while he uttered the humble words, *"Lord, do not hold this sin against them!"* (Acts 7:60). A humble suffering servant is a powerful testimony to the work of Christ in a believer's life. I wonder if the foreknowledge of Christ could see the future stoning of Stephen when from the hillside sermon He spoke these words: *"Blessed are those who are persecuted for the sake of righteousness, for theirs is the kingdom of Heaven"* The risen Savior certainly saw it. Stephen testified to this before his accusers, *"Behold. I see the heavens opened up and the Son of Man standing at the right hand of God"* (Acts 7:56).

10 – 9 – 8 – 7   Your Persecution Humility Score   4 - 3 – 2 - 1

Salt and Light (Matthew 5:13-16)

Let's continue to step through the Lord's lessons in His hillside sermon. I'm not sure how salt becomes tasteless, but Jesus declared that when it does, *"it is no longer good for anything."* In Matthew 5:13, Jesus called His followers *"salt of the earth."* There is a definite connection intended between those described in the beatitudes and those He then referred to as salt. Salt changes the things it touches and so do Christ's disciples who embody the passion and character of "The Beatitudes." Tasteless salt is what Christians become when the ingredient of humility is missing.

Verses 15 and 16 describe a life that shines *"before men in such a way that they may see your good works, and glorify your Father."* Jesus taught us to shine. We should not hide our light. Our light shines, however, for the purpose of giving God the glory. Pardon the mixture of metaphor, but when our pride claims glory for ourselves, our light becomes tasteless salt, *"no longer good for anything."*

The servant of Christ is salt and light; not light salt. We make the world a better and brighter place because Jesus has made our temperament tasty and our behavior bright. Keep it humble, or we become tasteless and dim.

10 – 9 – 8 – 7   Your Salt and Light Humility Score   4 – 3 – 2 - 1

You Fool! (Matthew 5:20-22)

Judging someone to have little or no value is an estimation produced by sinful pride. Jesus said, *". . . whoever says to his brother, 'you good for nothing,' shall be guilty before the supreme court; and whoever says, 'You fool,' shall be guilty enough to go into a fiery hell"* (Matthew 5:22). This is another lesson from the "Sermon on the Mount" that tells us about holding others in high regard. Living humbly means we cannot lift ourselves up and put others down. We judge others as valuable because they are of value to God, rather than judging them as worthless based upon their value to us. When we relate to others in the spirit of humility we will not call them good for nothing or fool, but will call them "ones who are loved by God."

Every person is created in the image of God, even those who have turned their back on Him and do not resemble the Creator's character. Judging anyone as good for nothing is an insult to the

Creator who made that person good for something. Our responsibility is to help people discover who God created them to be, not to convince them they are defective creatures. When we humble ourselves and step down from our pompous pedestal, we can begin to see others as having worth. In our humility we can stand together before God as fellow sinners who equally depend upon God for salvation, life, purpose, and hope.

10–9–8–7 Your Withholding Judgment Humility Score 4–3–2– 1

Humble Enough To Say, "I'M SORRY!"
Matthew (5:23-24)

Admitting a wrong can be a hard thing to do. It requires swallowing pride. It means we must say those three little chicken bone words "I was wrong" (chicken bone because they get stuck in our throats). Even if we believe people do not deserve our struggle, we must humble ourselves and sincerely apologize because it is right. Jesus expects us to be that kind of person. He even expects it when it is inconvenient. He said,

> *". . . if you are presenting your offering at the altar, and there remember that your brother has something against you, leave your offering there before the altar and go; first be reconciled to your brother, and then come and present your offering." (Matthew 5:24)*

Wow! Jesus spoke these words to a crowd, who had traveled via sandal, a great distance to the temple. Obeying Jesus' words could mean they would have to hot-foot it all the way home, apologize, and hoof it back to the temple to finish presenting their offering. Imagine walking home and arguing to ourselves all the way: "Is this person worth the walk?" But, that is how important reconciliation is. Our worship and sacrificial offerings are meaningful to God in proportion to the degree with which we are right with our fellow man. We must be humble enough to say, "I'm sorry." Only then can we humbly honor God, and appropriately worship Him.

Saying "I'm sorry" is often inconvenient, because we failed to say it when the wrong was first committed. It takes a while for us to admit to ourselves that we injured someone. When we finally get past our pride and accept that we owe an apology, the person we wronged is usually long gone. We must now plan an encounter and think of a way to get around to the subject of our transgression. It may take time and energy to follow through. Our "I'm sorry" may not be well received, but doing it is right and will at the very least strengthen our resolve to be a humble person.

10 – 9 – 8 – 7 Your Apologizing Humility Score 4 – 3 – 2 – 1

Looking and Lusting (Matthew 5:27-28)

It takes humility to set aside the fulfilling of selfish desires in favor of obedience to God. Jesus said, not only is the act of adultery a terrible sin, but looking at someone with sinful desire in our hearts is equally sinful. *"But I say to you that everyone who looks at a woman with lust for her has already . . ."* (Matthew 5:28). Sinful pride decides it is okay to think of someone as merely a sex object. Our lusting ignores any thought of damage we may do to a person, and any thought of harm we may do to our relationship with God. We are not seeing the person we are lusting after as a real person deserving respect and honor. We are not wishing God's best for them. We see them only as a thing to fill our selfish need for sexual fancy and fantasy.

Here is a reason pride is so dangerous: It always minimizes the worth of others. Once we see others as merely meat we allow ourselves to slice and dice, toast and roast, it becomes easy to call them a fool. Nothing within us cares to tell them, "I'm sorry." And, it becomes easy to believe that undressing them with our eyes and raping them in our minds is okay.

Christians must grow to a better understanding of the implications of Christ's words in Matthew 16:24, *"If anyone wishes to come after me, let him deny himself, and take up his cross, and follow me."* Choosing to deny ourselves those moments of sinful lust, and humbly bearing the cross of total commitment to Jesus, are involved in following Him. When we become humble, we can begin to see true beauty in every person. Each is a beautiful creation of Almighty God with meaning and purpose. Each can attain the sweet purity that is granted when washed in the blood of the Lamb. Seeing others this way raises the level of our responsibility to others, and our eyes from chest to face.

Pride persuades us to presume we are an exception to the commands of Christ. He said, *"Everyone who looks at a woman with lust for her has already committed adultery with her in his heart."* Sinful pride imagines those words to be unclear, situational, and not always applicable. How do we define the words *looks*, *with lust,* and *for her*? Pride will find a way to get permission for sinful desire. We must humble ourselves before we are able to accept what we don't want to hear, and to hear that our desire is unacceptable. Pride chooses rebellion. Humility chooses obedience.

10 – 9 – 8 – 7 Your Non-Lustful Humility Score 4 – 3 – 2 - 1

Giving Our Best (Matthew 5:38-42)

Jesus named five different kinds of people who confront us and bring out the worst in us: the abuser, an accuser, the bossy, the borrower, and an enemy. With each of these our human nature wants to respond from the law. *"An eye for an eye, and a tooth for a tooth"* (Matthew 5: 38). We put on our judicial robes, step up to the bench, drop the gavel and pronounce them guilty. We then determine their rightful penalty and swiftly execute their punishment. Jesus demanded that we respond differently to these despicable, detestable degenerates. Christians are to react not from our human nature, but from a nature that is of the Spirit. We respond not from the law, but from love. We humbly remove the judge's robes and put on a meek and quiet spirit. Remembering our own sins for which we are worthy of God's condemnation, we humble ourselves and allow God's love to define our reaction. Matthew 5:44 tells us to love and pray for those who are trying to get the best of us. We can give them our best: our love and prayers. We can weather the storms of insult, material loss, extreme burden, constant begging, and personal attack.

He mentioned first the abuser. *"Whoever slaps you on your right cheek, turn the other to him also"*(Matthew 5:39). Our pride responds, "No! I will not let anyone abuse me without immediate retribution!" We love movies where the underdog evens the score and blows away the big, bad face-slapper. "Go ahead. Make my day," we dare the one poised to slap. We have been taught to stand our ground, don't let anyone push us around, and show them who's boss.

Such a very different approach to the threat of violence is taught by our Savior and Lord. He teaches us a different kind of strength. Through the power of Jesus in our lives, we can control our passions so that we don't react with anger. We are able to confront meanness with humility. A slap elicits not a punch, but a prayer. Humility refuses to let anyone force us to be violent. When we practice a life of humility, we react to the good, bad, and the ugly about the same way. We are not different with friendly people than we are with slap-happy people. I think that is what Jesus teaches us. There are not times when it is okay to be mean-spirited. When someone, no matter who she is, slaps the living daylights out of us, without reason or cause, we remain humble, turn our face, and offer up the other cheek.

10–9–8–7 Your Facing Our Abusers Humility Score 4–3–2–1

So Sue Me! (Matthew 5:40)

After the abuser, Jesus mentions the accuser. *"If anyone wants to sue you and take your shirt, let him have your coat also."* Who would want to sue you for your shirt? Let's put this verse in the context of the day in which Jesus spoke. The shirt was an undergarment worn next to the skin, while the coat was the outer garment. These were very basic possessions. If a person is suing for your shirt, it is probably because you have nothing else of value. The person is being somewhat merciful by allowing you to keep your outer garment, but they would have to be a rascal to sue someone for one of their few remaining pieces of personal property. It is easy to see the humility required to do what Jesus asks in this verse. Standing before our accuser, we give the thing we are being sued for, and then to the amazement of the judge and jury, we strip off our outer garment, standing naked before our accuser, and hand over our last valued possession.

I'm not sure I fully comprehend the purpose of such an act beyond the need to live the humble life, unless we tie these words of Jesus to His words in verses 43 and 44. *"You have heard that it was said, 'You shall love your neighbor and hate your enemy.' But I say to you, love your enemies and pray for those who persecute you . . . ."* Christians must have such a humble spirit that, when we are attacked unmercifully in a court of law, we can demonstrate our non-attachment to material things and our love for our enemies by ensuring that the litigious one gets more than he has sought. We gain a greater capacity for humility because of it. The body of Christ gains in a far better witness through it. The litigator loses any satisfaction that might have been gained from it.

10–9–8–7 Your Facing Your Accusers Humility Score 4–3–2–1

The Extra Mile (Matthew 5:41)

"Go the extra mile." Familiar with the phrase? Today the phrase means for most people a willingness to do whatever it takes to get the job done. When Jesus talked about going the extra mile in His "Sermon on the Mount," he referred to instances in which the bossy Roman soldier was allowed by law to force a Jewish bystander to carry his military equipment as much as a mile. *"Whoever forces you to go one mile, go with him two"* (Matthew 5:41). Jesus is not alluding to some work ethic of serving above and beyond the call of duty. Our use of the phrase today is connected to achievement, high performance, and climbing the ladder of success. In the situation Jesus described, the Jew received no reward, had to travel the mile back to where he began, and probably complained the whole trip home about having to assist this foreign, oppressive, government employee. It is under these conditions that Jesus said, *"go with him two."*

We are called on to resist the prideful attitude that would insist the first mile was unjust, embarrassing, humiliating, and insulting. Pride would miss the opportunity afforded by the evil being done. Instead, Jesus expects us to have a humble spirit which allows us to take the demand in stride and go even further than expected. Humility enables us to turn a lemon into lemonade, misery into mirth, oppression into opportunity, a job into joy, and maybe a foe into a friend. Jesus asks us to make the better choice of accepting the hardship with an humble and good spirit, *"so that you may be sons of your Father who is in heaven; for He causes His sun to rise on the evil and the good . . ."* (Matthew 5:45).

10–9–8–7 Your Facing Bossiness Humility Score 4–3–2–1

The Borrower (Matthew 5:42)

Here is a lesson that immediately evokes a prideful reaction. We must carefully examine these words to be sure we are hearing what Jesus is saying. If we make wrong application of this one, we may be broke tomorrow. *"Give to him who asks of you, and do not turn away from him who wants to borrow from you."*

We don't need to worry that this command will make us poor. After we have torn out our right eye, cut off our right hand, turned the other cheek, given away our coat, and walked a second mile, we probably don't have much left to give (from verses 29-41). Keep this in mind. It is always a mistake to interpret any phrase or verse apart from the immediate and complete context. Before Jesus teaches us how to address the abuser, accuser, bossy, borrower, and enemy, His instruction is, *"Do not resist an evil person"* (Matthew 5:39). When an evil person demands that we become violent, turn the other cheek. When an evil person takes us to court to demand our shirt, give him also our coat. When an evil person forces us to go a mile, go with him two. When an evil person demands that we give him something or loan him something, do not refuse him.

Jesus teaches us to do the opposite of what our pride would do. Pride would react to the face slapper with anger and hate. Any response other than the one Jesus demands would allow evil to direct our actions. This is true of all evil persons mentioned, including the ones who demand that we give or loan something. The lesson on loaning does not mean that we must give a donation to every organization that asks, give a dollar to every beggar, loan money to every friend, or give your car keys to anyone who asks. It means when someone who intends to do evil demands something, do not resist with angry or evil actions. Do the opposite of what selfish and self-centered pride would do. Humbly yield to their demand.

10–9–8–7 Your Giving and Loaning Humility Score 4–3–2–1

Hidden Light (Matthew 6:1-4)

False humility refuses to do any good work, perform any public service, even to pray in public, because these acts draw attention to self. This attitude should be understood as laziness or lack of commitment rather than humility. If inactivity is a sincere attempt at humility, it is probably out of a misunderstanding of Jesus' warning against *"practicing your righteousness before men to be noticed by them"* (Matthew 6:1). In a chapter earlier,

Jesus pointed out the wrong in hiding our light under a basket and said, *"Let your light shine before men in such a way that they may see your good works, and glorify your Father who is in heaven"* (Matthew 5:16). The two instructions are not contradictory but rather complementary. Jesus didn't say, "Don't practice your righteousness before men." He said don't do it for the purpose of getting attention.

We are expected to let others see our light shining. God isn't glorified when the world sees nothing in His worshipers which cause them to take note. The world is accustomed to darkness. They will notice light. We are the wick which has been set on fire by God. We must stand tall so that others can see the light that is available to them. We must not blame a hidden light on humility. It is humility which enables us to hide the wick within the flame. Humility gladly holds up the light in the midst of darkness, so that others may see God.

Giving to the poor is a noble and right thing to do if done with unselfish humility. It is an example of a righteous act wrongly performed sometimes for applause or to increase one's community status. Jesus warned, *". . . do not sound a trumpet . . ."* (Matthew 6:2) when you help out a needy person. When it is obvious to us that someone wants recognition for their generosity, we are unimpressed by it. The insincerity of that kind of giving is shameful to us. We condemn the giver and the gift as gall and garbage. It is so easy to recognize wrong attitudes in others and so difficult to recognize it in ourselves. We hardly notice our own very pious attitude when lifting up the downtrodden, giving alms to bums, helping out a homeless shelter, collecting a couple of cans for the hungry, or just offering a smile to the smitten. We act as though we have done something great, when all we have done is what God requires of us. God expects us to care for the helpless. We have only done what is our duty to do when we reach out a hand to help.

We cannot take credit for having. We cannot claim to be better than the one who is in need. We can only humbly share what God has given us. A prideful attitude and a lack of humility when we offer assistance to anyone is robbing credit from God for resources He provided. If we are truly conscious of the source of all blessings, we will be humble and obedient to God whenever He chooses to provide for others with what we unworthily possess.

10–9–8–7 Your Helping The Needy Humility Score 4–3–2–1

The Secret to Prayer (6:5-13)

Humility was the difference between the prayer of the Pharisee and that of the tax collector in Luke 18. Jesus finished the story by saying of the tax collector, *"I tell you this man went down to his house justified rather than the other, for everyone who exalts himself will be humbled, but he who humbles himself shall be exalted"* (Luke 18:14). He taught this same principle in His "Sermon on the Mount." *"When you pray, you are not to be like the hypocrites; for they love to stand and pray . . . so that they may be seen by men"* (Matthew 6:5). Prayer is a big part of the humble life. It involves bowing before our magnificent and benevolent God, acknowledging His claim over our life, recognizing our total dependence upon His provision, knowing the need to repent daily, and yielding to His direction and council. Prayer is an exercise in humility. There is no real and sustained humility without prayer. Without humility, our prayers are attempts to address God as our equal.

To Solomon at the time of the dedication of the Temple, God spoke these wonderful words: *"If My people who are called by*

My name humble themselves and pray, and seek My face and turn from their wicked ways, then I will hear from heaven, will forgive their sin and will heal their land" (2 Chronicles 7:14). Sincere prayer and humility are inseparable. Prayer without humility is pharisaical. The secret to prayer is not prayer in secret. The secret to prayer is humility, which sometimes requires it be done in secret.

The model prayer, known to us as "The Lord's Prayer," is an example of humble praying (Matthew 6:9-13). We begin a humble prayer by acknowledging and demonstrating our lowly position before God. The person who begins prayer with, "Hey God!" or "It's me again, God" or anything similar, is addressing God with little respect, and a haughty spirit. That is not speaking to God; it is speaking at Him. The model prayer begins by acknowledging our relationship (*Our Father*), praising God's greatness (*hallowed be Your Name*), and recognizing His authority (*Your kingdom come . . . Your will be done*). When we fail to humble ourselves before God as we pray, we have misunderstood with whom we are speaking. Prayer is not getting God's attention. It is humbly giving our attention to God. Prayer is not wanting and wishing, but worshipping.

Enter prayer with full awareness of who God is, and the spirit of humility will permeate that prayer. Enter prayer as worshipper, and our attitude automatically becomes one of humbleness. A disciplined approach to prayer will take the time to address God properly, praise Him appropriately, and acknowledge His authority. With humility, our prayers for *"daily bread"* and *"forgive us our debts"* are not meaningless repetition. When we are meek, we relinquish our overestimation of self and pray, *"For Yours is the kingdom and the power and the glory forever. Amen."*

10 – 9 – 8 – 7   Your Humble Praying Score   4 – 3 – 2 – 1

A Personal Treasury (6:19-34)

When does saving an appropriate hedge against unexpected expenses or building income for retirement become storing up treasures on earth? In Matthew 6:19, Jesus may forbid the latter. I personally do not believe he forbids the former. He gives us three indicators to know when our financial practices have become *"storing up treasure on earth."* Each of these indicators could be considered a lack of humility. The first has to do with moths and rust. Treasure can become the thing we trust, replacing our trust in God. Jesus reminds us that our financial securities are untrustworthy. Be humble and trust God. Secondly, treasure very easily becomes the central focus of one's heart and life. *"Where your treasure is, there your heart will be also"* (Matthew 6:21). Be humble and love God. Thirdly, treasure takes control of our lives. Jesus warns, *"You cannot serve God and wealth"* (Matthew 6:24). Be humble and serve God. If we are trusting in, making a god of, or are a servant to our savings and financial holdings, then we are storing up earthly treasures and violating our Lord's command. Jesus' warning is clear. *"Do not store up for yourselves treasures on earth, ... but store up for yourselves treasures in heaven"* (Matthew 6:19-20).

Nineteen verses of the "Sermon on The Mount" (6:16-34) are spent teaching against an attachment to things. Material things can be an enemy of humility. They don't have to be, but they have great power to lure us away from the main thing. Seeing our eyes mesmerized by shiny stuff, Jesus takes our face in his hand and gently turns our head so that our eyes meet His and says, *"Seek first the kingdom and His righteousness, and all these things will be added to you"* (Matthew 6:33).

Our worry over what we will eat, drink, wear and a hundred other concerns reveal a pride that believes we are in control. We seem to think life depends on us and our ability to worry enough to meet all our needs. Worry is just another way of saying, "If it's going to be, it's up to me." That is sinful pride at its best. Humility hears the command of Jesus and trusts His words. *"Do not worry, . . . for your heavenly Father knows that you need all these things."* (Matthew 6:31-32). Literally and sincerely living a life of trusting God for our needs is an exercise in humility. When we pray, *"Give us this day our daily bread"* (Matthew 6:11), let that be a true prayer of faith in God.

10–9–8–7 Your Material Things Humility Score 4–3–2–1

The Golden Rule (7:7-12)

Contrary to popular belief, the golden rule is not – "He who has the gold, rules." Most people, even if they know nothing about the Bible or Christianity, they know what the golden rule is. You may not realize it, but it is the basic rule of humility. If humility is Philippians 2:3, *"Do nothing from selfishness or empty conceit, but with humility of mind let each of you regard one another as more important than himself,"* and if humility is Colossians 3:12, *"Put on a heart of compassion, kindness, humility, gentleness and patience,"* and if humility is Matthew 22:39, *"Love your neighbor as yourself,"* then Matthew 7:12, *"In everything treat people the same way you want them to treat you,"* is a basic rule for living the humble life. It is indeed, the golden rule! We ought not to think of it as a rule. It is a command. We are commanded to live humbly among friends and enemies. Only 49 verses earlier, Jesus taught us this: *"You have heard ... love your neighbor and hate your enemy. But I say to you, love your enemies ... "* (Matthew 5:43-44).

Given the context of the golden rule, Jesus expects us to treat our enemies the same way we want them to treat us. Now, that doesn't mean to treat them the way we suspect they will treat us. It doesn't say, treat them only if they ultimately return the favor. We know what it means. Even if a person is a scoundrel, and the sorriest person on earth, we are obliged to treat that person the way we would like to be treated. That is going to require a boat load of humility.

10 – 9 – 8 – 7 Your Golden Rule Humility Score 4 – 3 – 2 – 1

The Miracle Man (7:21-23)

Here is one last note from Jesus' amazing "Sermon On The-Mount." Are you aware that pride leads to an overestimation of self and an inability to take an honest look at one's true relationship with Jesus? Our Lord warns *"Not everyone who says to Me, 'Lord, Lord,' will enter the Kingdom of Heaven,"* (Matthew 7:21). Jesus explained how easy it is to identify His true followers, the righteous. Grapes do not grow on thorn bushes. Good trees bear good fruit, and bad ones bear bad fruit. His true disciples are those who bear good fruit. Prideful persons will object to the Lord's rejection of them by pointing to things they did for Jesus. *"Lord, did we not prophesy in Your name, and in Your name cast out demons, and in Your name perform may miracles?"*(Matthew 7:22). People may *use* the name of Jesus but never *know* Him as personal Lord and Savior. Pride focuses upon accomplishments for evidence. Humility focuses upon Christ and a personal love relationship with Him. We must humble ourselves before Him.

10–9–8–7 Your Honest Self-Assessment Humility Score 4–3–2 –1

Lessons from the Lord's lecture on the lofty ledge allow the learner to listen to the lamb and learn. We learn the blessedness of humility. We learn how to humbly live among men. We are taught the way to pray and fast with humility. The Lord teaches us a humble attitude toward possessions. And, we learn the end result of a life of pride. Read the "Sermon on the Mount" with humility on your mind, and every lesson will whisper, "Be humble!"

CHAPTER FIVE

JUDGE OR JOY

*"Do not judge so that you will not be judged.
For in the way you judge, you will be judged;"*
Matthew 7:1-2

❧

When we see someone's glaring flaw, we have a great urge to rush in and fix it. Are you like that? We think we must help people by correcting their eccentricities or strange behaviors. We can't resist it. We even back up our actions with Bible verses like Matthew 18:15, *"And if your brother sins, go and show him his fault in private; if he listens to you, you have won your brother."* With a Bible verse in our pocket, we feel authorized to judge the peculiarities of others, even when the verse isn't applicable. Most of the time we are neither reproving sin nor approaching persons in private. Instead, we are only critiquing personality and uniqueness. Sinful pride is present when we pick at someone's ways and think we must change them. It takes humility to allow others to be who they are. A humble person will accept the differentness of others and let them be. Humility can enjoy other people even though they aren't quite as perfect as we prefer them to be. Humility will turn a blind eye to the quirkiness of others and value them as unique creations of God. If we are only able to accept people after we have fixed them, we do not understand humility.

Judging others is habit forming. Soon we are unable to meet anyone without putting them through our personal examination, and if they fail, we feel responsible to do something. Humility can become habit, also. Practice enjoying people and letting go of the need to change them. Pray for that ability. Pray for a humility that can treat people who have laughable qualities and imperfections as more important than we are, even if they never ever change. Thank the Lord that He accepts us in all of our weirdness and wackiness.

But For the Grace of God

Of the many humble things we can do to keep from being critical of others, is a phrase used by a great preacher of the Church of England during the 1700's named George Whitefield. He was used by God during a period of history known as The First Great Awakening. Preaching with an emphasis on *grace,* George would point at a poor suffering soul and say, "There, but for the grace of God, go I." Unfortunately, this phrase is used with little regard to its humble intention. The divorced wife watches the new woman in her former husband's life and chuckles under her breathe, "There, but for the grace of God, go I." The millionaire to the beautiful blonde sitting next to him in his silver Mercedes as they drive by a scruffy man waving a cardboard sign that reads "homeless" arrogantly says, "There, but for the grace of God, go I."

If spoken with humility, this phrase can be a positively humble thing to say. A truly humble person is humble because they are certain that all blessings they enjoy are theirs only by the grace of God. If a few occurrences had been different, or if God had chosen to allow different events to take place in our lives, we might be in far worse condition than we are. Seeing any person in a course of life which we would not want to experience, we should humbly declare, "There, but for the grace of God, go I." The humble use of this phrase should remind us of the truth of it. The reality of the phrase should cause us to respond to any person, whom we might wrongly judge, with a more humble attitude.

We are usually inaccurate in our judgment of our own condition. We think having a high paying job, authority and power, notoriety, and lots of expensive stuff is the blessed life. The truth is, the person with a simple life, wearing inexpensive clothing, riding a bus to a mediocre job may observe someone in a much higher financial bracket and think, "There, but for the grace of God, go I." God's sovereign choices for our lives acknowledged by this humble phrase should calm our judgmental reflex and raise our humility quotient.

Humblievable

We all tend to make snap judgments of people, don't we? We briefly observe a person's posture, apparel, expression, and imperfect appearance and feel we have downloaded enough data to accurately define them. In a matter of nanoseconds we are able to blurt out our indubitable deduction – "Nerd!" Each person within our view is tagged as they undergo scrupulous inspection: loser, redneck, blonde, dunce, or truculent. We pride ourselves on our ability to point out a person's character and worth.

Are we able to recognize a humble person just as easily? Is it as easy to identify the humble as it is to identify other character types? If so, we could assume that there are some recognizable indicators of humility. We know a person is a redneck by the fishing lure hanging from his cap. We are certain of the dunce when we see her super-innocent expressions. We can postulate that a girl is blonde, just because she's blonde. It may be a little more difficult to judge someone to be humble. Posture that may indicate humility may actually be revealing a dunderhead. Apparel that gives a first impression of humility may be merely a sign of a country bumpkin. A quiet, unassuming person may seem humble but in reality be a flaming lunatic. We may be able to discern who is not humble, but not able to single out who is.

Maybe a truly humble person is so rare that we lack experience that would help us know one when we see one. Maybe we have become so suspect of all people that we don't expect to find anyone who is truly humble. Persons who seem humble are later found to be lacking in humility, so we assume all will fail the test. We expect that all people are flawed. No one can convince us that our snap judgments are incorrect. None could be so full of integrity and consistently good that we could pin the humble tag on them. Where is the man or woman who is humblievable? Where is the man or woman who can restore our belief that there are truly humble people in the world? Is being humblievable something anyone would even care to be?

All this ranting is intended to illustrate how ridiculous are our attempts to judge others. We cannot make accurate judgments, because we cannot know a person's mind and heart. Yet we make this our favorite pastime and hobby. We think it is funny to fire off a few zingers at each passerby. We prefer to judge rather than to see others as God's unique creation.

Throw Some Dirt

I can not imagine myself killing someone. Believing I have the right to take someone's life would be for me an arrogant act of self-righteousness and pride. It would mean that I have judged that person to be no longer worthy of life and myself to be righteous enough to make and carry out that judgment. It could mean, of course, that I have judged some action of theirs to be a threat to me or others, and that the threat must be squashed even if doing so requires they be terminated. I wonder how closely we come every day to making the kind of self-righteous judgments that would allow us to pump some lead into at least one or two deserving sinners who cross our path.

There are reprobates and degenerates everywhere, even in church. Just look around some Sunday when the congregation sings "It is well with my soul" and see who is choking on those words. Guilty persons should be singled out. Drag that adulterous woman out into the open, so we can end her threat to my society. Pass out the stones. Pick up some big stones, or at least some little ones. If not stones, we could at least throw some dirt, can't we? Can we throw a few insults? Come on, we must do something. Aren't we justified in our judgment of her? Do we not have a responsibility to point out his sin? Show them the door. They don't belong here.

Judging others is an act of sinful pride. Jesus calls us to a life of humility with His convicting offer, *"He who is without sin among you, let him be the first to throw a stone at her"* (John 8:7). Humility requires that I put down the stone and stop promoting my own self-righteousness. Humility recognizes there is a plank in my eye which renders me ineligible to remove the speck in the eye of another. *"How can you say to your brother, 'Let me take the speck out of your eye,' and behold, the log is in your own eye?"* (Matthew 7:4). We would never seriously consider killing someone, yet we readily condemn them to hell. Self-centered pride needs to view others with low regard, so it makes harsh, snap judgments. Humility judges people as deserving high regard.

Microscopic Humility

Our motivation to act, not the action itself, determines whether we are acting humbly or otherwise. When we let someone take the last piece of pie, is our motivation meekness or poor self-worth? When we curb our conversation to allow someone to change the direction of the discourse, are we being humble or hateful? If we try to hide in the shadows when in a crowd, is humility our game or righteous reputation fabrication? What motivates our actions? Do we sincerely wish for humility? Do we want it because we want to be like Christ, or are we only eager to raise our spiritual fitness score? Questioning our motivation is a step in the right direction. If we are honest, we may be able to stop the charade. It is better to admit a lack of humility than to fool ourselves into thinking we are humble. Recognizing when we are not truly humble is an aid to building true humility.

There are two dangers to developing an awareness of wrong motivation. First, we may begin to think we can accurately judge the motivations of others. Involvement in this will always interfere with our own humility. Second, we may begin to overjudge our personal motivations and give up ever trying to be humble. We must scrutinize our own motives under a magnifying glass and not a microscope. We must observe the motives of others through the wrong end of binoculars. It is a good thing to be devoted to a life of humility, but that virtue must never become a mechanism to destroy the joy of our salvation or to measure the value of others. When it does, we are no longer living the humble life.

I intended the following poem as sarcasm. I wrote it years ago while in college. I'm not sure if I was feeling guilty about judging others or feeling like I was being overly scrutinized by my peers. I believe the poem portrays the attitude of some people I know, but I would be judging them if I were to claim that.

Church Bats

A guest preacher one Sunday had to cope with a bat flying overhead and a congregation of bat gazers. Every unique moment becomes an opportunity to learn more about humbleness. With each new event the humble person ought to ask, "How can I think and act with humility in this situation?" The quickest way to answer that is to determine if we are responding with selfish or selfless motives. If we are reacting selfishly then we are not acting humbly. If we are thinking about how circumstances are bothering me, upsetting me, inconveniencing me, worrying me, disturbing me, costing me, damaging my image, or making me look bad, then we will not act humbly. If we are thinking about how circumstances will affect others, harm others, discourage others, worry others, or humiliate others, then it may be that we will act humbly. But again, if we are acting out of concern for others, but hope to gain something for ourselves in the process, then our action is again not likely humble.

It is difficult to remove consideration for ourselves from our thinking and acting. As I sat in the audience trying to ignore the bat while completely horrified at what I was witnessing, my first response was to pray, "Please, Dear God, give that bat a massive heart attack. Now!" I then did that thing where you stare intently at the object of ire expecting your glare to magically cause the bat to burst into flames. It didn't. Next, I imagined myself running across the top of church members' heads like a China-man in the movie "Crouching Tiger, Hidden Dragon" until I soared upward and snatched the bat out of thin air. It would be awesome if I could do something cool to fix our bat problem. It wouldn't be very humble, though. Living for Christ isn't about being cool or awesome. It is about being a bond-servant for Jesus and loving those whom God created and loves.

In my desire to destroy the bothersome bat, I failed to recognize the flying interference as a work of wonder by Almighty God. A humble reaction to this unusual happening might be to absorb the sermon, while appreciating all God's creatures to include the only one present with the gift of self-levitation (the bat). After all, if I destroy this distraction, what happens next week when I am the cause of the commotion? Humility involves valuing life regardless of how that life may interfere with my plans, my path, or my peace. Our pride wants to judge some people or things as unworthy of existing. Our humility enables us to reach out to the most detestable, despicable and distasteful lives around us, and care about them . . . even if they should fly over and poop on our head. That would be another opportunity to learn more about being humble.

I Have a Dream

Prejudice is a pride thing. If we are humble, we are able to listen without prejudice to someone whom pride would ignore. One person, plus humility, minus prejudice equals an ability to hear (1 + H − P = hearing). One person, minus humility, plus prejudice equals deafness (1 − H + P = deafness). Okay, that may sound dumb, but the point is this: Our ability to understand others is limited when we pre-judge. If we listen without pre-judging people, and form our opinion of what they say on what we fully hear, we stand to get understanding which we might otherwise completely miss. I wonder how much greater all of our understanding would be if we were all a bit more humble.

We receive the thoughts and ideas of others with a passel of pride and prejudice. For example, you have already prejudged me for using the word *passel*. It just means *a large amount*. A lack of humility results in the whacky white person misunderstanding the oppressed black person. The wise Democrat can't hear the much wiser Republican. The Israeli can't hear the Palestinian. The female won't listen to the stronger gender. The younger generation has closed an ear to all the elderly. The pro-choice crowd can't hear the screaming of the unborn child. Yankees can't listen to anyone with a southern drawl. Global warming advocates won't listen to any scientists who interpret the data differently. Balaam wouldn't listen to his donkey. Ludwig Van Beethoven couldn't hear his piano. I can't hear a dog whistle. And, none of us are going to hear a single thing others are trying to say unless we hawk-up a little humility.

A humble spirit can curb one's prejudging long enough for a fresh thought to slip from the lips of an otherwise objectionable source to enter our ears and penetrate the gray matter inside our fat heads. Once the idea finds a wrinkle in which to rest, it is up to the possessor of the new idea to determine its usefulness. I could get more technical, but I won't. Actually, if I am honest and humble about it, my technical acumen is suspect.

All I really know is this: I have a dream, that one day our nation will rise up and live out the true meaning of humility. I have a dream that one day in the red hills of the south, the sons of

Martin Luther King, Jr. and the sons of George Wallace can stop waving flags and fists to sit down at the table of Tyler Perry. I have a dream that my two little children will one day live in a nation where they will not be judged by the color of their skin but by the humus of their humility. I have a dream that one day the kind of pride and prejudice that leads to blindness and deafness will be replaced by the kind of meekness and humbleness that opens our eyes and ears and makes it possible for us to see and hear each other as never before. Maybe then will come the day when all of God's children will be able to sing with new meaning: "But if you're thinking about my baby, it don't matter if . . ." (oops not that one). We will all sing with new meaning:

> We all know that people are the same wherever you go
> There's good and bad in everyone
> We learn to live, we learn to give each other
> What we need to survive together alive.
> Ebony and Ivory
> Live together in perfect harmony
> Side by side on my piano keyboard
> Oh Lord, why don't we?[15]

Judging Judy

The ease with which we quickly judge the stranger on the street is a testimony to the ample arrogance and pride present within us. The discipline required to avoid judging is an example of the strength and power of humility. One must be very humble to resist the urge to judge. Jesus asks, *"Why do you look*

---

[15] 1982 Hit song by Paul McCartney, sung by Stevie Wonder. Featured on McCartney's album *Tug of War*.

at the speck that is in your brother's eye, but do not notice the log that is in your own eye?" (Matthew 7:4). I think we do that because our pride is interested in making us look good and has discovered an easy way to do that - make others look bad. Pride enables us to build up ourselves by tearing down others.

Disciplining ourselves to stop judging is an exercise in humility. "I'm not going to judge. I'm not going to judge!" But, just when I tell myself, "I'm not going to judge," a young freakish looking teenager comes in to view with his hand on the crotch of his pants to keep them from falling down. "I am not going to judge. I will not judge him. I am withholding judgment." I realize that I must try to have a positive thought about the teen to draw my focus away from his contrary appearance. In the midst of my moment of misery a middle-aged woman appears. Oh great! This woman looks like she has been living on a diet of Pop-Tarts and Twinkies. Her hugeness is not going to cause me to judge. "I am not going to judge. I cannot judge her. It's not going to happen. Breathe deeply. Look away." Ooops! I didn't mean for my eyes to become fixed on a co-worker with whom I have had numerous problems. I am not going to judge even though a video tape is playing countless scenes in my head. "Stop the tape! I will not judge. I will not judge!!!"

Children - let's just watch the children. They are small and sweet. There isn't anything about them that tempts me to judge. They are playful and beautiful, most of the time. Sometimes they can be way too rowdy and loud and disrespectful. That is because their parents don't teach them right from wrong, or they are divorced, or they never married, or they're vegetarians. Most parents are too selfish or too lazy to give their children the kind of love and spankings they deserve. That is why children become teens with their pants around their knees, or they put on pounds and pounds of ugly flesh, or become contentious coworkers . . . But, I am not going to judge. I'm not. I'm too humble for that. Wow! Trying to be humble is soooo hard!

The Enemy of Worship

We are such critics of everything we see and hear that it is sometimes difficult to draw a worshipful experience from any moment in church. The singer is too pitchy. The music is too loud. The minister's sentence structure is bad. The platform furniture is not arranged symmetrically. The temperature is too hot. The Pastor's tie is too flashy. The sermon notes on the screen have a misspelled word. The bulletin notes are too busy. The person behind me keeps clearing her throat. On and on we can go with our observations until we fail to get in touch with any sense of God's presence or hear any rush of angels' wings. The Spirit may be speaking, but our critical clatter drowns Him out. Is it possible that pride is at work robbing us of real worship?

Pride is an insidious enemy of the worshipping soul. It sets an impossibly high standard which must be met in order to have a satisfactory worship experience. It looks at detail and detects fine departures from perfection. It isn't pleased when entertainers and aesthetics don't measure up. The result is that we go through motions without any emotion. We play the part of worshipper but never become one. No connection is made with the one we claim to be worshipping. We go away from a worship hour blaming the preacher, the music, people around us, the fly that wouldn't leave us alone, or the building temperature. The real culprit is very often our own prideful spirit. We fail to humble our hearts before almighty God. We fail to recognize the absolute necessity of humility in worship. So, our head and heart are never in it. It isn't the sermon or the sanctuary that is cold; it is us.

When we learn to enter worship with a humility that refuses to be judgmental, we will learn to worship. We have not yet shed the pride and put on humility until we are able to listen to the worst singer on earth singing "Amazing Grace," with heartfelt praise to God during and after the presentation of it. Until we can rejoice when the Word of God is preached just because it is being preached, without picking apart the instrument of God, we are all too full of ourselves and not ready for praise time. If all things were perfect - singing, bulletin, worship center, people, preacher, aesthetics and ambiance - we would run the risk of praising and loving all those elements instead of the Lord.

Satan tempted Jesus in the desert by offering Him a perfect world. He took Him to a very high mountain and showed Him all the kingdoms of the world and their glory. *"All these things I'll give you,"* Satan said, *"If you will fall down and worship me"* (Matthew 4:9). Satan tells Christians, "Keep searching. One day you will find a perfect church with glorious buildings, amazing music, and the kind of preaching you enjoy." Satan's lie is that satisfaction is found in things. It is not. Satisfaction is found only in the Lord.

Jesus responded to Satan's promises, *"You shall worship the Lord your God, and serve Him only"* (Matthew 4:10). We all love good music and good preaching. It is, however, amazing how much better the preaching gets and the singing sounds, when it is God whom we are worshipping and not some ideal church of our imagination. Humility is the key. The Psalmist directs us this way: *"Come, let us worship and bow down, Let us kneel before the Lord our Maker. For He is our God, And we are the people of His pasture and the sheep of His hand"* (Psalm 95:6-7).

Reacting To Aggravation

How we receive abuse from others will influence our humble position before God. Andrew Murray, a great preacher and writer of the nineteenth century, said we should "look upon every fellow man who tries or vexes you as a means of grace to humble you. Use every opportunity of humbling yourself before your fellow men as a help to abide humbly before God."[16]

The way we interpret any situation will determine our reaction to it. Imagine seeing every challenge, confrontation, irritation, persecution, and aggravation that comes from others as opportunity to be humble. Our reaction to vexation or provocation is not usually such a calm and controlled one. We don't take lightly to an offense. Our normal reaction is a defensive one. We attack back. We can't let others walk all over us, can we? How would that make us look? We might appear weak, meek, and . . . humble. Part of the problem we have with living the humble life is that we think of the humble reaction as a weak one. Try it, however, and we realize great strength is required. A humble response to life is the path our Lord calls us to follow.

As a servant of the Lord, we are meant to react to every situation and every person with humility. We react to praise with humility. We react to success with humility. We must react to the blessings of God with humility. We can react to pain and suffering with humility, too. We also react to destructive and abusive people with humility. Any reaction other than a humble one will be under the direction of sinful pride. We can't let that happen. We must learn to look at every fellow man who tries or vexes us as a work of grace to humble us. Reacting to provocation with humility will inevitably lead us to give thanks to God in every-

---

[16] Andrew Murray, *Humility* (Gainesville, FL: Bridge-Logos, 2000), 61.

thing. And the giving of thanks to God in everything will replace our normal first response to judge.

> *"But you, why do you judge your brother? Or you again, why do you regard your brother with contempt? For we will all stand before the judgment seat of God. For it is written, As I live, says the Lord, every knee shall bow to Me, and every tongue shall give praise to God. So then each one of us will give an account of himself to God. Therefore let us not judge one another anymore, . . ."* *(Romans 14:10-13).*

CHAPTER SIX

HUMBLE BIBLE PEOPLE

"And you shall remember all the way which the Lord your God has led you in the wilderness these forty years, that He might humble you, testing you, to know what was in your heart, whether you would keep His commandments or not. And He humble you and let you be hungry, and fed you with manna ..." Deuteronomy 8:2-3

֍

Humility is not a wimpy, spineless thing. The kind of humility described by the Bible requires strength and bravery. It is an attitude of lowliness that is willing to suffer any loss and carry any cross because the self has bowed in obedience before the will of God. The prophet Amos humbly asserted, *"I am not a prophet, nor am I the son of a prophet; for I am a herdsman and a grower of sycamore figs. But the Lord took me from following the flock and the Lord said to me, Go prophesy to My people Israel"* (Amos 7:14-15). A humble Amos left his home in Judah to announce God's judgment on Israel. There he delivered not a mild-mannered message, but a powerful reprimand preceded by, *"Thus says the Lord!"* Serving God requires a bold humility, not a cowardly pride.

Daniel, in defiance of the law of King Darius, *"continued kneeling on his knees three times a day, praying and giving thanks before his God . . ."* (Daniel 6:10). Daniel knew his humility would land him in the lion's den. It took great courage to choose humility. His humble obedience provided the event by which God's authority and power would close the mouths of lions and rewrite a royal edict.

It wasn't pride by which David volunteered to face Goliath. That would have been foolish pride. The smaller, lesser equipped son of Jesse drew his courage from a humble heart gripped by the greatness of God. *"The Lord who delivered me from the paw of the lion and from the paw of the bear, He will deliver me from the hand of this Philistine"* (1 Samuel 17:37).

David wrote this bold assertion to God. *"The boastful shall not stand before Your eyes; . . ."* (Psalm 5:5). His Psalms are riddled throughout with a humble approach to the throne of God. Psalm 91 is the confession of a courageous yet humble servant.

> *"He who dwells in the shelter of the Most High will abide in the shadow of the Almighty. I will say to the Lord, My refuge and my fortress, My God, in whom I trust! For it is He who delivers you from the snare of the trapper and from the deadly pestilence. He will cover you with His pinions, and under His wings you may seek refuge; His faithfulness is a shield and bulwark." Psalm 91:1-4*

Those words do not come from someone who hides in fear and hopes for God's deliverance. They come from one who humbly dared to face great challenges for a God with whom he had walked through both green pastures and dark valleys. The kind of humility David, Daniel, and Amos had is not for the fainthearted. They had an attitude that was prepared to follow The Lord down whatever path He chose. Lives like these humble Bible people are not for the skittish or squeamish. It is for daring, dedicated, devoted followers of Christ. *"Therefore, humble yourselves under the mighty hand of God. . ."* (1 Peter 5:6).

Noah

Imagine being humble when everyone else is not. Imagine a world where everyone is arrogant and conceited except for you. In Noah's day, evil reigned. The Bible says, *"The Lord saw the wickedness of man was great on the earth, and that every intent of the thoughts of his heart was only evil continually"* (Genesis 6:5).

The words of his father, Lamech, when Noah was born may reveal a prevalent attitude that encouraged the contempt for God and wickedness of the people during Noah's life. The words of this one hundred and eighty-two year old regarding his new son were, *"This one will give us rest from our work and from the toil of our hands arising from the ground which the Lord has cursed"* (Genesis 5:29). Lamech's statement is meant to be an expression of hope. I wonder if it actually reveals a common anger and resentment of the people toward God. Long years harboring hate for the expulsion from Eden and the punishment all had since endured, hardened their hearts. They reacted with bitterness instead of humbleness. Their arrogance toward God brought about His ultimate decision. *"The Lord was sorry he made man on the earth"* (Genesis 6:6).

"But Noah found favor in the eyes of the Lord" (Genesis 6:8). How was Noah able to live a life that pleased God in an age when no one else did? The prophet Micah answered the question, *"What does the Lord require of you but to do justice, to love kindness, and to walk humbly with your God?"* (Micah 6:8). Noah chose that life, and God saw humility in the heart of him.

God gave Noah blueprints for a great ship of salvation and commanded him to build it. The Bible simply says, *"According to all that God had commanded him, so he did"* (Genesis 6:22). Then God instructed him to enter the ark with every kind of animal. Once again, after God's instructions the Bible records, *"Noah did according to all that the Lord commanded him"* (Genesis 7:5). Then the rain and the floods came, covered the earth, and destroyed all life outside of the ark. Months later, Noah looked outside and found that the surface of the ground was dry. An arrogant person would have thought to himself, *I have survived the great flood. God chose me above all others to replenish the earth. I am The Man!* The prideful man would have leaped from the ark and planted his foot on the ground declaring, "I am king of the world!" But Noah waited until God gave the command. His first act out of the ark was to build an altar and worship. That is humility.

God still wants to walk with humble men and women. He delights in those who will receive blessings of success and high position with humility and whose first thoughts are to give Him praise.

Humbleton

When I set up a new blog site and showed it to my wife, the first thing she saw was the first blog's title: *The Most Humble Man*. The title appeared below my picture so it is no surprise she would think I was pinning that title on myself. It was actually about Moses, but why would she think it humorous if I were writing about me? Am I not a very humble man? Is the fact of my humility hidden from her? But of course, I am so humble that I would never draw attention to my own humility. I would not dare point to it, or indicate when I have acted humbly. I'm too humble for that. It would be nice if my wife recognized my humbleness, but she might be so astonished once she became aware of it that she would begin some litany of praise which would make it difficult for me to remain humble. It is probably best that she not fully understand what a humbleton I am. A humbleton? Sounds rather like simpleton, which would be okay because the truly humble would not be so proud as to be offended by whatever he or she were called. Humility does not need a special title or attention. Humility is its own reward and has no need for applause.

Here is the *most humble man* reference, as found in The New English Bible in Numbers 12:3. "*Moses was in fact a man of great humility, the most humble man on earth.*" Since the book of Numbers was written by Moses, I am sure he wrote that statement about himself only because everyone acknowledged it to be true. It was just a fact. It was probably like the deacon, as the congregation was shaking hands with the preacher at the end of morning worship, who watched as one of the church members kept getting back in line so that she could give another negative comment on the sermon. After the third time passing the poor pastor with her critique, the deacon offered some encouragement, "Don't pay any attention to what she says, Pastor. She only repeats what she hears others say." Perhaps Moses was only repeating the words that kept circulating among the masses. He was not being conceited, but only recording historical detail.

Charisma

Humility played an important role in the life of Moses, both in his obedience to God and in the acceptance of His leadership by God's people. Humility is a valuable trait for leaders. People much more readily follow leaders who are humble. John Maxwell says the quality that draws other people to a leader can be summarized in one word: CHARISMA. In his book, *Be A People Person*, he says, "The potential to be charismatic lies within each of us, but first we must remove hindrances from the development of this important personality characteristic."[17] The very first hindrance he gives is *pride*. People do not like to follow one who is arrogant and prideful. Maxwell explains that pride is a roadblock to charisma.

We are not drawn to people who are full of themselves. We are, however, drawn to people who are humble. Humble people are approachable. They are touchable. They are warm and real. Those who are pride-full repel us. We aren't sure we can trust them. We are challenged by their conceit to find a flaw, a chink in their armor. Out of our disgust for their self-centeredness, we hope they fail. They may think they have charisma, but what they have is *obnoxia*.

If we are alarmed by selfishness and charmed by selflessness, what sort of persons should we want to be? If we enjoy people, want their company, and want them to follow our leadership, we will learn to be humble. If we want to influence people, humility will be among the qualities which we covet and practice. We will despise egotism and egoism when we see it in ourselves as much as we dislike it when we find it in others. We will be drawn more toward those in whom we find humility and influenced less by those with swagger and gall. As we grow more humble, we will become more honest and authentic, and grasp more fully what Maxwell means by *charisma*.

---

[17] John C. Maxwell, *Be A People Person* (Colorado Springs: Chariot Victor Publishing, 1994), 33.

The Humility of Job

Humility is the broth of our chicken soup, the cheese on our macaroni, the cinnamon on our breakfast roll. It is that ingredient in our character that makes more enjoyable the rest of our character. Courage and fortitude are wonderful when mixed with a little humility. A high IQ is much more easily tolerated when humility is present. Wealth is not a part of character, of course, but humility certainly is refreshing when it accompanies wealth. A humble millionaire is much more approachable and real than a conceited one.

Job was a wealthy man. Job's possessions included 7000 sheep, 3000 camels, 500 yoke of oxen, and 500 female donkeys. The story of Job begins by enumerating all he had and then adds, *". . . and that man was the greatest of all the men of the east."* The virtue for which Job is best known is patience and secondly his perseverance. Is it possible that Job's greatness actually lies more in his humility? During a conversation I had recently, an employee responded to my diatribe with, "That doesn't sound like truth to me." Describing Job as humble may not sound like truth, but a little investigation into Job's responses to life may convince us to see Job differently.

Job's Response to Catastrophe

After God allowed Satan to afflict Job, there are lengthy chapters where Job carped, complained and was quite negative. While this is true, it doesn't mean he wasn't humble in the midst of his moaning and groaning. When he questioned what God was doing, Job did so in much the same way Jesus did when he cried out from His position of agony on the cross, *"My God, why have you forsaken me?"* (Matthew 27:46). No one suggests that Jesus was without humility at that moment. They both spoke honestly with God regarding their suffering and agony.

Job spoke boldly to his friends about God. Out of intense pain and anguish, Job wished for a moment to stand before God in a courtroom where he could declare his innocence and God's injustice. Throughout Job's protest there is evidence of his humility. We hear him scream at his friends about God, *"Let Him remove His rod from me, and let not dread of Him terrify me. Then I would speak and not fear Him; But I am not like that in myself"* (9:34-35). Though he would like to be bold enough before God that he could speak however harshly he wanted, the fear of the Lord was still within the heart of Job. No measure of pain and suffering could drive Job to cast fear to the wind and become disrespectful or irreverent to God. I think Job is an example of the exhortation, *"Be angry and yet do not sin"* (Ephesians 4:26). He was clearly angry about his plight but never cursed God or acted hatefully toward Him. What a challenge it is for any of us when suffering more than our fair share to express our true feelings to God while maintaining a submissive and lowly posture toward Him!

The initial response of Job to catastrophic loss and misery was, *"The Lord gave and the Lord has taken away. Blessed be the name of the Lord"* (1:21). He said to his wife, *"Shall we indeed accept good from God and not accept adversity?"* (2:10). Job didn't understand why God would allow so much bad to happen. He wanted some explanation from God, but he humbly accepted his lot. He later declared, *"I know that my Redeemer lives . . . Even after my skin is destroyed, yet from my flesh I shall see God . . ."* (19:25-26).

Job's Response to Critricism

The friends of Job were pretty brutal in their attempt at explaining Job's troubles. They came to his side to comfort him, but after staring at him without saying a word for seven days, they piously insisted that Job somehow deserved what God had dished out. Job humbly sat in his pitiful condition and listened to Eliphaz for a total of 113 verses, Bildad for 49, Zophar for 49, and Elihu for a whopping 165 verses. Job was critical of his friends. He called them *"sorry comforters"* (16:2). He responded to them by saying, *"How long will you torment me and crush me with your words?"* (19:2). Yet he listened, perhaps hoping that something the friends shared would make sense and provide answers.

God in His mercy interrupted the insanely long exhortation of Elihu, and after a painfully intimate conversation with Job, He scolded Eliphaz and the other two. *"My wrath is kindled against you . . . because you have not spoken of Me what is right as My servant Job has"* (42:7). God knew Job well. He told the friends that Job would pray for them and, *"I will accept him so that I may not do with you according to your folly"* (42:8). To pray for friends who accuse and abuse instead of comfort and console while you are in a crisis requires a spirit of humility. What a guy!

Job's Response to Correction

Our God is an awesome God. On Mount Sinai there was smoke *"because the Lord descended upon it in fire."* The whole mountain shook as Moses met God on the mountaintop. Moses spoke *"and God answered him with thunder"* (Exodus 19:19).

God responded to Job's tirade *"out of the whirlwind"* (38:1). *"Where were you when I laid the foundation of the earth? Tell Me, if you have understanding . . . Have you ever in your life commanded the morning and caused the dawn to know its place?"* (38:4,12). God gave no answer to Job's "Why me, Lord?" Job received instead a sharp reminder of the power and authority of God. *"Do you have an arm like God, and can you thunder with a voice like His?"* (40:9).

When our hearts are prideful, even when we are confronted by almighty God, we want to argue back and defend our actions and attitudes. Job's humble heart is revealed once again as he responded to God's thunder. *"I retract, and I repent in dust and ashes"* (42:6). Job, to Satan's chagrin, was still humble after losing family and all his possessions. Satan insisted that if God would *"touch his bone and his flesh; he will curse You and Your face"* (2:5). Job took the worst life can dish out and remained a man of integrity, faith, and humility. His humble reaction to God's exhortation does not come after he is healed and helped, but while he is still suffering loss and writhing in pain. God knew Job well that he would stand Satan's testing.

Job's Response to Consolation

"The Lord restored the fortunes of Job when he prayed for his friends, and the Lord increased all that Job had two-fold. . . . The Lord blessed the latter days of Job more than his beginning . . ." (42:10,12). We have no evidence that Job remained humble after his ordeal was finished and he returned to prosperity. We can make a pretty good guess. Job was humble with wealth in the beginning. He was humble during horrible misery, unjust criticism by so-called friends, and under the dis-

ciplinary voice of God. Job must have known the truth of Peter's words, *"Humble yourselves under the mighty hand of God that He may exalt you at the proper time"* (1 Peter 5:6). It is a lesson we learn from the life of Job. It is a lesson in humility.

Isaiah's Experience

The prophet Isaiah's personal experience with God, recorded in chapter six, provides insight into elements of humility. The story enables us to understand the process of humbling ourselves before God. The process is more about an encounter than an exercise of human will. Humility is not merely being humble, but the act of moving closer to the Lord. Humbling ourselves before God involves right thought and attitude. Just as was true for Isaiah, real humility takes place when we have:

A collision with God's awesomeness,
A vision of God's holiness,
An admission of utter filthiness,
The elation of God's forgiveness,
Attention to God's voiced address,
The question of our willingness,
A call to mission for God's graciousness,
A believer filled with humble eagerness,
Commissioned as God's ordained evangelist.

John The Baptizer

One of the best biblical examples of humility is John the Baptizer. In John we find strong, fearless service combined with selflessness. Humility is not an excuse to be timid and cowardly. It is the denial of self that boldly falls on a grenade or steps in front of a bullet. The mission is not about self. The humble one is not in the spotlight to draw attention to herself, but rather steps willingly into the light out of devotion to God.

John had the sort of humility that could unashamedly and unshakably say to the Pharisees and Sadducees, *"You brood of vipers, who warned you to flee from the wrath to come?"* (Matthew 3:7), and yet respond to questions about himself with, *"I am a voice of one crying in the wilderness, make straight the way of the Lord"* (John 1:23). He was just a voice. He would not claim to be a great prophet, but only a voice. There is nothing here to see, he said, only words to hear. He didn't claim to be a great orator, only a lonely shout in the outback.

His humility was evident. While courageously confronting Herod with the shocking sin of having his brother's wife (Mark 6:18), John would confess to the crowd that he was not fit to remove the sandals of the one he was sent to announce (Matthew 3:11). In his humility, John declared, *"I baptize you with water but one has come who will baptize you with the Holy Spirit and with fire"* (Luke 3:16).

Humility will say, "It's not about me." If we question God's plan to use us to do His will, then we have fixed the focus on ourselves. If we refuse to accept God's purpose for us because we feel unworthy, then we have decided it is more about us than about God. If we let the fear of getting our heads cut off keep us from delivering God's message, then we have let the moment become about us. Humility doesn't stop to ask, "But what about me?" Self is not the consideration. It's all about God. We are only voices. We must decrease, and He must increase. We are but humble servants, crying everywhere God sends us, "Behold the Lamb of God."

Mother of Jesus

Christians are sometimes so careful to avoid elevating Mary to the status of deity that we fail to give her appropriate praise for her extraordinary faith and uncommon humility. When I get to heaven, after the first thousand or so years at the feet of Jesus, I would like to spend some time enjoying the presence of the earthly mother of Jesus. Humility is obvious as this young girl accepted the angel's message and willingly placed her life at God's disposal. She was so overwhelmed by the blessedness of being chosen to serve God that she launched into a praise known as The *Magnificat* (Luke 1:46-55). Allow me to paraphrase.

> And Mary said:
> Wow! My soul and my spirit are giddy with praise.
> My savior rewarded my humility.
> Forever people will know how blessed I am.
> God Almighty blessed me.
> The Holy One is merciful to those who fear Him.
> He brings down the proud and lifts up the humble.
> He fills the hungry and ignores the rich.
> His mercy is with Israel just as he has said to our fathers.

Mary knew that it was humility that placed her in God's favor. She was humble, not because she was poor, or young, or from humble circumstances. She was humble because her God was the master of her life, and she chose to honor Him by her humble life. God chose her because he knew that through all the events to follow, she would remain a humble soul.

Humiliation and Humility

Humiliation is not the same as humility. When we do or say something which results in being humiliated, the experience may be humbling to us, but we are not therefore humble. The feeling of humiliation may, in fact, indicate the presence of sinful pride. Why, we must ask, did the situation cause a feeling of humiliation? Was it because the moment made us look unfavorable or appear to be someone less than we believed ourselves to be in the eyes of those present? When truly humble, we are not so concerned about what others think that some critical act or disparaging word would cause us to be overcome by a feeling of humiliation. The humble life is actually a liberating one. The truly humble person does not suffer humiliation as does the one who is not acquainted with humility.

The difference between humiliation and humility is illustrated in the parable of The Good Samaritan. The man who fell among robbers and was stripped and beaten was consequently stripped of pride and humiliated. On the other hand, the Good Samaritan made a choice to set aside his pride and became a humble caregiver. Which of these is true? Is a spirit of humility a prerequisite to compassion and mercy, or does compassion and mercy arouse a spirit of humility? It is interesting to note how many good things are either made possible by humbleness or are dependent upon humility. In some cases, the good thing and humility are interdependent. The Good Samaritan is the shining biblical example of a compassionate caregiver and the perfect picture of humility. Both the priest and Levite who arrived earlier at the bloody scene were either too occupied or too dignified, and their hearts too petrified to provide care. Preoccupation with one's own stuff and a view of one's self that minimizes the value of others is a definition of sinful pride.

Persons who invest themselves in the care of others, as the Good Samaritan did, are usually models of humility. Clothed in humility, they are able to see hurt, pain, and need. Their humble spirit enables them to selflessly act to comfort and care for persons whom others would rather avoid and ignore. People whose days are spent at home caring for a sick wife, mother, or other relative, or are in a care-giving profession at hospital, hospice, or nursing home, are the humble heroes of our society. Most of them are uninterested in recognition and praise. Their humble spirit enables them to tirelessly care for impaired, impotent, and infirm. Only the humble could gently and compassionately wipe away the blood, or change the adult diaper, or mop up the vomit, or bathe, or feed, or listen to long laments from unlovely, unproductive, and sometimes ungrateful persons. Jesus attributes honor to these compassionately humble caregivers. After He tells their story, represented by the Good Samaritan, He issues a directive. Jesus says to all of us, *"Go and do the same"* (Luke 10:37).

Peter and Cornelius

Cornelius was the Gentile through whom God demonstrated His intention to save more than Jews. God convinced Peter, by a vision and by Peter's encounter with this centurion, that *"In every nation the man who fears Him and does what is right is welcome to Him"* (Acts 10:35). The Apostles and brethren in Judea reprimanded Peter for going to the house of an uncircumcised man. Peter's testimony, however, convinced them that *"God has granted to the Gentiles also the repentance that leads to life"* (Acts 11:18). Of course, The Holy Spirit had something to do with all that convincing.

This Gentile, who was the central figure of one of the longest stories in the book of Acts, was a humble man. He is a great example of one who has strength, respect, authority and humility. His story begins with this description: *"a devout man and one who feared God . . . and gave many alms to the Jewish people and prayed to God continually"* (Acts 10:2). I believe all of this spells humility. God hears the prayers of the humble. God answered the prayer of this humble soldier and sent first an angel, then a high-ranking Apostle of Jesus.

Cornelius was a man who lacked arrogance and conceit. When Peter responded to his invitation and arrived at his house, this member of an elite battalion fell at the feet of a Jewish fisherman. And this was not a private scene. Excited about the message Peter was bringing, he had gathered a large group of family and friends. Before this crowd of onlookers, Cornelius, without any reservation, treated the Jew with extreme respect and high regard. He was a humble man ready for God to be his Lord and Savior.

Timothy!!!

I wonder about Paul's child in the faith, Timothy. Did he suffer from a misunderstanding of humility? I wonder because of certain personal instructions Paul gave in the two letters addressed to Timothy. Christians sometimes think that humility means to be passive, unassertive, and even inactive. They think humbleness means non-resistance. If that is what Timothy thought, then we can understand some of the coaching Paul gave him. Paul urged in his first letter, *"This command I entrust to you, Timothy, my son, in accordance with the prophecies previously made concerning you, that by them you fight the good fight"* (1:18). Paul ended the letter with the same urging, *"Fight the good fight of faith; take hold of the eternal life to which you were called . . ."* (6:12). The second letter to Timothy immediately picked up this same theme. *"God has not given us a spirit of timidity, but of power and love and discipline"* (1:7). In the second chapter of that letter, he called upon Timothy to *"be strong in the grace that is in Christ Jesus"* (2:1), and then charged him to *"suffer hardship with me, as a good soldier of Christ Jesus"* (2:3). Paul finished the second letter with further instruction for Timothy to operate from a position of confident strength. *"I solemnly charge you in the presence of God and of Christ Jesus, who is to judge the living and the dead, and by His appearing and His kingdom: preach the word; be ready in season and out of season; reprove, rebuke, exhort, with great patience and instruction"* (4:1-2).

Another misunderstanding by Christians is that humility requires us to forego achievement, initiative, and excellence. Once again, I suspect Timothy needed Paul to teach him what humility really means. Paul clearly described humble behavior throughout both letters to Timothy, but needed to challenge Timothy to step up to the plate and hit a home run. In his first letter, Paul said, *"Let no one look down on your youthfulness, but rather . . . show yourself an example of those who believe"* (4:12). He followed with, *"Pay close attention to yourself and to your teaching; persevere in these things, for as you do this you will ensure salvation both for yourself and for those who hear you"* (4:16). In his second letter Paul admonished, *"Be diligent to present yourself approved to God as a workman who does not need to be ashamed"* (2:15).

Paul was a humble man who taught Timothy by word and example how to be humble. He put his hands on Timothy's shoulders, shook him a little, and said, "Pay attention, Son." He then proceeded to explain some things about humility. The unselfish, devoted, humble life for a bond-slave of Jesus Christ is not one of weakness and failure. It is a life of strength and diligence. I trust Paul will forgive me if I put unintended words into his mouth. But, I can almost hear him firmly speaking to Timothy: Get your lazy self up, stop listening to foolishness (2:2:23), stop doubting your calling and God's gift within you, *"Endure hardship, do the work of an evangelist, fulfill your ministry!"* (2:4:5). It is a lesson many Christians need to hear about the humble life.

Mothers

On Mother's Day I heard a local news anchor comment that motherhood is hard. I thought about that and decided part of the reason this is true is the constant requirement for moms to be humble. Very good moms, I think, are those who succeed at carrying out their mom duties with humility. I have always heard things said about mothers like the little boy who confessed, "When there is only one piece of pie left, mom isn't hungry." Humility enables mom to carefully step over dirty clothes, toys, books, bags and unidentifiable stuff, say nothing about the mess, and kiss the little darling goodnight. With humility mom will quietly endure the hurtful words from her child who is fighting for independence long before he or she is mature enough to handle it. Humility makes it possible for mom to continue to work at a low-paying, unpleasant job, day after day, year after year, so her son or daughter, who will never fully appreciate her sacrifice, can finish college. Out of humility comes the sweet, kind, loving words spoken over the phone to her supposedly adult child who finally calls after weeks or months of irresponsible neglect. But that's mom, caring more about her children than they will ever care for her or she for herself. That is love with an armful of humility. Jochebed, the mother of Moses, is just one example of mothers who humbly sacrificed themselves for the welfare of their precious children. The only way to save her baby boy from death was to give him up to Pharaoh's daughter. She then volunteered to nurse the boy without giving away her identity as mother. Silently she cared for the young child and eventually gave him up again to grow up in Pharaoh's house. Only another mother can fully understand the pain and sacrifice and strength involved in what Jochebed did.

The Bible is full of stories of other moms who provide us with great examples of humility. Motherhood isn't easy. It is never easy to be humble, not even for a mother. The good ones find humility an asset to motherhood and make it part of their character. When love, faith, and hope are placed in the pressure cooker of life, and the sweet smell of humility becomes apparent, there is probably a mother standing close by.

The Harlot

"There was a woman in the city who was a sinner." That is the way the story begins in Luke 7 detailing one of the most beautiful examples of humility in the Bible. This woman wet the feet of Jesus with her tears, wiped them with her hair, kissed them, and anointed them with perfume. An act of love? Yes! And that love is expressed with a great show of humility. There are acts of love that are not wrapped in humility. We much prefer to show affection while at the same time maintaining a digni-

fied posture. When a show of love is delivered with humility, that expression of love has its greatest impact. Jesus was moved by this woman's offering. He explained that her act indicated far greater love for Him than the hospitality and meal given Him by Simon the Pharisee in whose house this event took place.

Love for Jesus is always best expressed when our heart is humble. Our service to Jesus is always a better offering when performed humbly. Our prayers are always best communicated by humble lips. The activities of our lives are always better witnesses of our love for Jesus when they are humble acts. Our pledge of commitment to Jesus is always more sincere when made with a meek and humble spirit. Becoming more like Jesus is to become more humble. Jesus described himself in this way: *"Come to Me, all who are weary and heavy laden, and I will give you rest. Take My yoke upon you and learn from Me, for I am gentle and humble in heart, and you will find rest for your souls"* (Matthew 11:28-29).

CHAPTER SEVEN

LET'S GET READY TO HUMBLE

"Therefore, putting aside all filthiness and all that remains of wickedness, in humility receive the word implanted, which is able to save your souls."
James 1:21

☙❧

Only a little investigation into scripture should reveal to every Christian the preeminence of humility among the prescribed attitudes of believers. Our Bible is replete with references to and examples of the role of humility. In *The Pillars of Christian Character*, John MacArthur says, "This attitude is at the very center of the Christian life. It is the foundation of all graces . . ."[18] Humility is not an attitude which a follower of Christ can take as an elective. It is a prerequisite to the life of a disciple.

It would be wonderful if all Christians were overwhelmed with a desire to be humble. Imagine! Humble church leadership with faithful believers following their example, meeting together in a true spirit of humility to humbly worship Almighty God, and humbly accept our commission to serve Him. What is necessary for that vision to become reality? C.S. Lewis wrote, "If anyone would like to acquire humility, I can, I think, tell him the first step. The first step is to realize that one is proud. And a big-

---

[18] John F. Macarthur, *The Pillars of Christian Character* (Wheaton: Crossway Books, 1998), 29.

gish step, too. At least, nothing whatever can be done before it. If you think you are not conceited, it means you are very conceited indeed."[19]

Look at the *"if"* in this quotation. Admittedly, I am taking this quote a little out of context, but I wish Lewis had chosen different words. "If anyone would like to acquire humility," could instead have been worded, "while everyone is endeavoring to acquire humility," or, "in our united quest to acquire humility." He didn't choose those words because it wouldn't have made sense. There are not many people clamoring to acquire this virtue. Humility is not a characteristic that we naturally aspire to after examining a long list of noteworthy characteristics. It is one, instead, which some are resigned to become only after scripture has convicted them that they ought to be humble.

Franklin's 13

Past generations have held a higher opinion of the value of humility than we find today. A few centuries ago, writers mentioned humility and other virtues in the context of the common belief and thought of their day. There are some classic treatises. Dante completed *The Divine Comedy* around 1320 AD in which he describes carvings on the walls in the lowest level of purgatory depicting stories of humility for the prideful residents of that level to view. Geoffrey Chaucer, writing around 1390 AD, provided a long discussion of pride and humility in "The Parson's Tale" of *The Canterbury Tales*. References to humility pop up in the writings of Shakespeare, Confucius, and Dickens.

---

[19] *The Joyful Christian*, 127 Readings From C.S.Lewis (New York: Macmillan Publishing Co., Inc., 1977) 144

Dr. Benjamin Franklin's *Poor Richard's Almanack* was published each year from 1732 to 1758. In a collection of his proverbs and wisdom from that publication is found Franklin's *Thirteen Virtues*. We don't know if he listed them in an order of importance, but the last virtue on the list is *humility*. I'm glad it made the list. After naming each virtue, Ben offers a few words of definition, e.g. "Temperance: Eat not to dullness. Drink not to elevation." When he comes to "humility" he simply describes it with: "Imitate Jesus and Socrates."[20]

Please note: I am deliberately not addressing the subject of the humility of Socrates. Someone else can write that book. I only wish that humility came at the head of Franklin's list rather than the tail. Most lists of virtues by various sophists and philosophizers will not place humility near the top. Don't let that dissuade us from our quest to study this virtue. While some people might consider it mere quartz in the realm of gems, we will find that it is a jewel to be placed at the center of our crown surrounded by the less precious ones. One of Ben Franklin's aphorisms states, "A cipher and humility make the other figures and virtues of tenfold value."[21] A cipher (zero) added to the number 5 makes it 50, thus 10 times its value. That is what Franklin says happens when we add humility to our character. Without a doubt, this remarkable man considered humility a virtue to be favored. It is one which adds value to every other virtue. It, above others, should be highly coveted.

---

[20] *Poor Richard's Almanack* (Mount Vernon, NY: Peter Pauper Press, 1983), 73.

[21] Ibid., 71.

The Rule of Saint Benedict

Christians have studied and practiced humility from the earliest days of Christ's church. About 1500 years ago, one man listed 12 degrees of humility. These are found in a collection of his beliefs and instructions known as "The Rule of Saint Benedict." St Benedict of Nursia lived from 480 to 543 AD. He founded the monastery that became the roots of the Roman Catholic Church's monastic system. His rules were written for the domestic life of laymen who wished to live as fully as possible the Christian life presented in the Gospels. Chapter seven is titled, "De Humilitate." I have condensed St Benedict's 12 steps of humility from a translation by Terrence Kardong. I confess that I will not personally practice all twelve of these. I mainly recount them as a matter of historical record on the subject of humility and for whatever enlightenment they may provide. Here we go:

First step: Keep the fear of God always before your eyes. (Psalm 36:1-3).

Second step: Take no delight in satisfying desires out of love for your own way. *"I have come down from heaven, not to do My own will, but the will of Him who sent Me."* (John 6:38)

Third step: Submit to your superior in all obedience for love of God. *"He* [Jesus] *humbled himself by becoming obedient to the point of death."* (Philippians 2:8)

Fourth step: When obedience involves harsh, hostile things or even injustice of some sort, embrace them patiently with no outcry. (Matthew 10:22)

Fifth step: Reveal through humble confession to your abbot all evil thoughts that enter the heart, as well as the evils secretly committed. *"Confess your sins to one another, and pray for one another so that you may be healed."* (James 5:16)

Sixth step: Be content with low and dishonorable treatment and regarding all that is commanded you, think of yourself as a bad and worthless worker. (Luke 17:7-10)

Seventh step: Not only confess with your tongue, but also believe with all your heart that you are lower and less honorable than all the rest. *"But I am a worm and not a man, a reproach of men and despised by the people."* (Psalm 22:6)

Eighth step: Do nothing except what is encouraged by the common rule of the monastery and the example of the veteran members of the community.

Ninth step: Hold your tongue from speaking, and out of love for silence do not speak until someone asks a question. *"When there are many words, transgression is unavoidable, but he who restrains his lips is wise."* (Proverbs 10:19)

Tenth step: Don't be quick to laugh at the slightest provocation. *"Sorrow is better than laughter."* (Ecclesiastes 7:3-6)

Eleventh Step: When a monk speaks at all, he does so gently and without laughter, humbly and seriously, with few and careful words.

Twelfth Step: When a monk's humility is not only in his heart, it is apparent in his very body to those who see him. . . (Luke 18:13)[22]

What Saint Benedict provides is a description of extreme, monastic humility. We must accept it and respect it for what it is. It is, however, a somewhat scary, run the other way and don't look back humility. This is what we imagine to be required of us if we are to be humble. This is "clamp my tongue in a vice and slap me silly" humility. Please hold on to the arms of your chair while we tip-toe past St. Benedict and find our way along a less extreme path of humility.

Broken Bread and Poured-Out Wine

There is a beautiful representation of humility found as a re-occurring theme in the well-known devotional, *My Utmost For His Highest*. Oswald Chambers calls upon Christians to become "broken bread and poured-out wine." Learning what that means will give us insights into the humble life. Here are excerpts from Ozzy.

Feb 15: Am I willing to be broken bread and poured-out wine for Him? Am I willing to be of no value to this age or this life except for one purpose and one alone – to be used to disciple men and women to the Lord Jesus Christ?

May 15: We are here to submit to His will so that He may work through us what He wants. Once we realize this, He will

---

[22] Terrence G. Kardong, *Benedict's Rule, A Translation and Commentary* (Collegeville, Minn: The Liturgical Press, 1996), 132-135.

make us broken bread and poured-out wine with which to feed and nourish others.

Jul 15: Quit praying about yourself, and spend your life for the sake of others as the bondservant of Jesus. That is the true meaning of being broken bread and poured-out wine in real life.

Nov 15: When we are consciously aware of being used as broken bread and poured-out wine, we have yet another level to reach – a level where all awareness of ourselves and of what God is doing through us is completely eliminated. A saint is never consciously a saint – a saint is consciously dependent on God.[23]

Oswald Chambers provides a slightly different representation. St Benedict's humility requires an extremely harsh, self-annihilating, self-deprecating, misery-loving sort of humbleness. Chambers' humility involves surrender, giving, accepting and being resigned to the will of God. The difference between these two depictions is a little like the difference between the acts of *respect* and *awe*.

R.E.S.P.E.C.T.

The dictionary definition of *awe* is "respectful fear inspired by authority." Another definition is "a feeling of amazement." The other word, *respect,* is defined both as "admiration for a person or entity because of perceived merit," or "high or special regard." Allow me to suggest that we might choose to attribute high regard to anyone and everyone because of our high regard

---

[23] James Reimann, ed. *My Utmost for His Highest: An Updated Edition In Today's Language*, Oswald Chambers (Michigan: Discovery House Publishers, 1992.)

for all human life. Contrary to the definition, our high regard for others, and thus our *respect*, does not require that others have any special merit. *Awe*, on the other hand, is usually accompanied by a perception of someone's greatness or value greater than ourselves. We stand in *awe* before Almighty God. We may be in *awe* of a few special people. We have *respect* for many people. We are in *awe* of only a few.

I am making this distinction in order to make a point about humility. We do not need to be in *awe* of someone in order to be humble before them. We sometimes think that humility requires that we stand in *awe* of others and demean ourselves. When the Bible instructs us to regard others more highly than ourselves (Philippians 2:3), we are not being asked to tremble before them and do away with ourselves. We are directed to *respect* them. We value everyone, but not at the expense of our own value.

Jesus was ready to meet any need, expend his personal time, value every person whether high ranking or outcast, and offer himself up for others. He did not ever rank himself as unimportant, unworthy, or unnecessary. He was always humble but never overtaken with *awe* regarding anyone. He respected everyone, put others ahead of his own needs, but never considered his own needs as irrelevant or insignificant. He is our example of true humility. We are asked to *"love your neighbor as yourself"* (Matthew 22:39). In fact, Jesus says this is the greatest commandment, second only to the commandment to love God. These two commandments require that we love God, others, and ourselves.

Many Christians love God and others but have so suppressed, judged, and sought to extinguish self that there is not much of self to love. There isn't even much of self left with which to love God and others. Humility is not the obliteration of self, and it is not the elevation of others to "god" status. Humility is a healthy self-worth and self-appreciation that chooses to hold others with high regard. Humility wants the best for others. Humility places others ahead of self, not because self doesn't deserve to be first, but because self is committed to service and forgets about itself in favor of others. Humility is not fueled by burning up one's self. Humility is energized by a vision of the Son of God: meeting, mending, comforting, calling, correcting, touching, telling, suffering, serving, giving, helping, healing, loving, leading, listening, disciplining, defending, doing, and dying. That vision accentuates our own value to value others. It also accentuates the value we should place on **true humility**.

Humility Poll

Pride is deadly obvious during occasions when we are chatting with each other. You may not identify the presence of pride and humility during those casual discussions among friends, but you are aware that sometimes the dialogue is pleasant and other times painful. Often the difference is attributable to the presence of pride or the absence of humility. So, you're having a conversation and you are trying to be humblesome. How are you doing? Make a speedy personal appraisal of your deportment using this checklist.

1. Is at least 40 percent of the conversation not about me?
2. Am I truly interested in what others are saying?
3. Have I periodically relinquished control of the conversation?
4. Have there been periods of 3 to 4 minutes when I said nothing?
5. Am I responding with proper emotion to what others are saying? (i.e., joy, surprise, righteous indignation)

6. Was I careful not to interrupt anyone in the middle of their thought or story?
7. When others interrupted me, was I quietly forgiving and unbothered by it?
8. Have I avoided negative body language? (i.e., staring at the ceiling, arms crossed like a referee's delay of game penalty, fingers shaped like an "L" placed on the forehead)
9. Have I extended any compliment, praise, thanks, or offers to assist?
10. Have I carefully limited unsolicited advice?
11. Have I observed the traffic signs displayed by others in the conversation? (i.e., stop, go, yield, time out, slow children, quiet zone, personal space: do not come any closer!)

If you can answer "Yes" to all of these, you are indeed most humble. Keep it up. Humility will win friends and make your enemies envious. If you answered "No" to any one of these, you have a problem. Examine each question for which you answered "No." You now have the wonderful opportunity to grow in your humility and to correct a flaw which others could see, but no one has been brave enough to show you.

Am I Great And Worthy of Your Praise?

Is it possible to be humble and not feel *good* about being humble? The biblical directives of 1 Peter 5:5 and James 4:9 to *"humble yourselves,"* and of Ephesians 4:2 to *"walk... with all humility,"* say nothing about feelings. Feelings are unreliable and should not be allowed to control us. It is very possible to be humble and not get good feelings from it. Humility is a choice. It is a way of behaving which does not always leave us feeling warm and appreciated. It isn't like pride. Sometimes we have people around us who make it easy for us to give into the fleshly and carnal tendency to be puffed-up. They stimulate our egos by their gracious praise and flattery. It feels good for someone to think highly of us. It feels real good. Our egos are more often battered and bruised by others than they are fed. Our pride wants a nice emotional massage now and then. We deserve it, don't we? Flatterers are a godsend. Our self-worth may not survive without them. As adulation is received, the pleasure of it leaves us longing for more. We seek out those people who will build us up and who will bring us joy by inflating our ego. That joy soon turns into a need.

Applause and plaudits are addictive. Our egos become dependent upon them. We find that we cannot function without them. Accompanied by compliments and kudos, we carry on quite well. But when deprived of them for a short while, we crash and burn. Feelings become more important to us than doing what is right. We can't help it. We must have more and more accolades and commendations.

Humility doesn't provide for us like pride does. Without the freedom to toot our own horn or to enjoy someone else tooting it, we do commendable things that no one sees and most may not consider tootable. The selfless work of humility allows others to take the credit which might more appropriately belong to us. That doesn't feel good. Humility can feel like we are alone and unappreciated. After a few attempts at humility that leave us feeling unloved, the next time we are called upon to be humble, we may respond with, "I'm just not feeling it." We want humility to be rewarded by some pleasurable feeling. If it doesn't bring on a good feeling, why should we want to be humble?

Feelings. Nothing more than feelings. When will we finally break free from the slavery of self-glory and choose obedience to God? When will we break away from the grip of pride so that we can *"Walk . . . with all humility?"* It is time to *"Humble yourselves under the mighty hand of God."* It is okay not to feel good while being humble. Just be humble. *"God is opposed to the proud but gives grace to the humble"* (James 4:6). It is time for us to find out more about being what God wants us to be.

Humbling God's People

The Bible contains many stories of God's work to humble His people. God demonstrated his power over Pharaoh with ten compellingly powerful plagues. After finally forfeiting his firstborn, Pharaoh was sufficiently humbled to allow God's people to depart the land of Egypt. What followed was forty years of wandering in the desert for the Children of Israel. God's plan was to humble his people before they crossed over into the Promised Land. He explained that purpose to His people through His servant Moses.

> *"You shall remember all the way which the Lord your God has led you in the wilderness these forty years, that He might humble you, testing you, to know what was in your heart, whether you would keep His commandments or not. He humbled you and let you be hungry, and fed you with manna . . . Thus you are to know in your heart that the Lord your God was disciplining you just as a man disciplines his son." (Deuteronomy 8:2,3,5)*

On one occasion during the desert period, to further discipline His people, God sent fiery serpents to bite them because they grumbled and complained against Him. Having been humbled, *"The people came to Moses and said, 'We have sinned, because we have spoken against the Lord and you . . .'"* (Numbers 21:7).

It was often necessary for God to do some humbling. On many occasions, God refused to continue with His plan for His people until they became humble. When Naaman, the Captain of the Army of Aram, finally became humble enough to dip himself seven times in the Jordan River, God healed his leprosy. For Solomon, the process and purpose of being made humble was delivered by God at the dedication of Solomon's temple's.

> *"If I shut up the heavens so that there is no rain, or if I command the locust to devour the land, or if I send pestilence among My people, and My people who are called by My name humble themselves and pray and seek My face and turn from their wicked ways, then I will hear from heaven, will forgive their sin and will heal their land."* 2 Chronicles 7:13 – 14.

Only when God locked Jonah away for three days in the belly of a great fish, was Jonah humble to the point of obedience. Obedience should not wait for the humbling actions of God. His desire is that we humble ourselves, not wait to be made humble. Jesus said, *"Whoever then humbles himself as this child, he is the greatest in the kingdom of heaven"* (Matthew 18:4). James reminded us, *"Humble yourselves in the presence of the Lord, and He will exalt you"* (James 4:10). Peter said this again in 1 Peter 5:6, *"God is opposed to the proud, but gives grace to the humble. Therefore humble yourselves ..."*

Oh, what blessings have been delayed, what direction has gone un-given, what provision has been out of reach, what experience has been missed, what prayer is yet unanswered, because we have yet to humble ourselves before a God who may be on the brink of bringing us through the painful process of humbling and disciplining? If only we could open our ears to hear the voice of God speaking to us as He did to Pharaoh, *"How long will you refuse to humble yourself before Me? . . . For if you refuse . . . I will bring locusts . . ."* (Exodus 10:3-4). We must become humble before God completes that sentence for us. Let's get ready to be humble!

Humility, Gentleness and Also Patience

Our worthy walk with God involves three foundational characteristics which are basic to Christian living: humility, gentleness, and patience. I find it interesting that the second and third characteristic cannot be present without the first, and both become indicators of the presence of the first. All three perform best when linked together. A worthy walk that is prepared to *"show tolerance for others in love,"* and is readily *"diligent to preserve the unity of the Spirit in the bond of peace,"* is one that begins with humility, gentleness and patience.

> *"Therefore I, the prisoner of the Lord, implore you to walk in a manner worthy of the calling with which you have been called, with all humility and gentleness, with patience, showing tolerance for one another in love, being diligent to preserve the unity of the Spirit in the bond of peace" Ephesians 4:1-3.*

"So, as those who have been chosen of God, holy and beloved, put on a heart of compassion, kindness, humility, gentleness and patience; . . ." Colossians 3:12.

Scripture repeatedly admonishes us to be humble and to walk in humility. We are warned over and again of the outcome of prideful living. We may choose to escape the continual bombardment of this message by withdrawing from reading God's Word. The act of allowing the Bible to grow dusty is itself a decision rooted in pride. When we don't want to be humble, we stop listening to the voice of God. His voice will only repeat the same message. *"Humble yourselves."* Our pride ignores the alarm, pulls the pillow over our ears so that we can go back to sleep, and wonders at the ashes around us when we wake up later.

Three Things Lacking

When pride comes, disgrace comes too. (Proverbs 11:2)
The pride of heart always deceives you. (Jeremiah 49:16)
Pride breeds quarrels, precedes a fall. (Proverbs 13:10; 16:18)
It doesn't leave God any room at all. (Psalm 10:4)
God hates the arrogant, hates the proud. (Proverbs 8:3)
God hates and will punish this woeful crowd. (Proverbs 16:5)
Three things lacking across the nations:
Humility, gentleness, and also patience. (Colossians 3:12)

A Worthy Walk

The person who replies to Paul's imploring us *"to walk in a worthy manner"* with the assertion that she is totally unworthy of that calling, misses Paul's point while fooling no one by her thinly disguised pride. None of us is worthy of the calling with which we have been called, but all of us are urged toward behavior that renders us more deserving than believers who seem to have forgotten the character of the one whom we are called to follow. *"If indeed you have heard Him and have been taught in Him, just as truth is in Jesus,"* Paul preaches, *"Put on the new self, which in the likeness of God has been created in righteousness and holiness of the truth"* (Ephesians 4:21-24).

The worthy walk is humbly obedient. When a servant of Christ leaves humility out of his character, he has misunderstood the meaning of servanthood. When a member of the body of Christ stops being humble, she is in danger of believing she can function without the body. When the evangelist, pastor, or teacher falls from the ranks of the humble, he or she will become ineffective in equipping, building up, and in moving Christ's church toward unity (Ephesians 4:11-13). Throughout chapter four of Ephesians there is a description of the worthy walk and many reminders that Christians must be committed to living a life of **true humility**.

And Also Patience

An argument starts, or just continues,
Breaking hearts and bones and sinews.
No pause for civil problem solving,
No notice of the love dissolving.

Curse the pride that fans the fire.
Curse the ever deepening mire.
Three things conquer pride's creations:
Humility, gentleness, and also patience.

One drink began a loathsome journey,
Ending on a cold basement gurney.
No cry for help, no quiet contrition,
No addiction to alcohol admission.
Curse the pride that hides the pain,
Curse the choice to die in vain.
Three things break up pride's fixations:
Humility, gentleness, and also patience.

Lust for power, wealth and pleasure,
Successful living by man's measure.
No need to reach up for God's hand,
No rock foundation, only sand.
Curse the pride that drives man's greed,
Curse the sad self-centered creed.
Three things silence life's flirtations:
Humility, gentleness, and also patience.

Serve One Another

Christian service demands humility. All the words of Christ and New Testament scripture regarding the matter of ministry and service imply the presence of humility. When we serve God, the church, and others, we must humble ourselves in order to do it. Pride impedes our serving. Humility frees us to serve. Paul, in Galatians 5:13, says that we should, *". . . through love serve one another. For the whole law is fulfilled in one word, in the statement, You shall love your neighbor as yourself."* The biblical call to service is a command to highly regard others and expend energy and time on someone other than ourselves. Where Christians are found actively serving, we find a humble community of believers who probably are experiencing a high degree of unity and harmony. Usually, Christians who do not participate in service are Christians with a low level of humility and a high level of church family dysfunction. Humility and service are intimately related. Christians who desire personal growth in humble living are well on their way when they step through the door of service. Serving brings us to the feet of the ones whom we serve, to wash and gently touch their need. That is true humility.

> *"Then the King will say to those on His right, 'Come, you who are blessed of My Father, inherit the kingdom prepared for you from the foundation of the world. For I was hungry, and you gave Me something to eat; I was thirsty, and you gave Me something to drink; I was a stranger, and you invited Me in; naked, and you clothes Me; I was sick, and you visited Me; I was in prison, and you came to Me.' Then the righteous will answer Him, 'Lord, when did we see You hungry, and feed You, or thirsty . . . , a stranger . . . , or naked . . . , sick or in prison . . . .?' The King will answer and say to them, 'Truly I say to you, to the extent that you did it to one of these brothers of Mine, even the least of them, you did it to Me.'" (Matthew 25:34-40)*

Humble Town

Humble Town is where God wants us to live. James 4:9 says, *"Humble yourselves in the presence of the Lord, and He will exalt you."* Philippians 2:3 says, *"Do nothing from selfishness or empty conceit, but with humility of mind let each of you regard one another as more important . . . ."* Jesus says in Matthew 18:4, *"Whoever then humbles himself as this child, he is the greatest in the kingdom of heaven."*

There is no question that humility is to be readily apparent in the life of those who are followers of Jesus. Humility paves the way for our obedience. It is a prerequisite to confession, devotion and worship. Why then does humility receive so little promotion? The most popular character traits in our society are those which are contrary to a spirit of humility. It is with a desire to promote the value and significance of humility in the Christian life that this book attempts to be a billboard to campaign for humility. That road sign will read: *"He leads the humble in justice, and He teaches the humble His way"* (Psalm 25:9).

God expected the Hebrew people to live in humble town. The Law, special days, feasts, and ritual, all had an element of humility in them. The annual Day of Atonement provided an opportunity to return to humble living.

> *"And this shall be a permanent statute for you: in the seventh month, on the tenth day of the month, you shall humble your souls, and not do any work, whether the native, or the alien who sojourns among you; for it is on this day that atonement shall be made for you to cleanse you; you shall be clean from all your sins before the LORD. It is to be a Sabbath of solemn rest for you, that you may humble your souls; it is a permanent statue." (Leviticus 16:29-31)*

Is it necessary to cease all labor to become humble? It surely must help. We know that busyness is an enemy of relationships. Just as we can become too busy for each other, we can be too busy for God. The Psalmist records God saying, *"Cease striving and know that I am God"* (Psalm 46:10). Perhaps the reason The Lord, my Shepherd, *"makes me lie down in green pastures"* and *"leads me beside quiet waters,"* is that we must be at rest for us to humbly let Him *"restore my soul"* (Psalm 23:3). When we are too busy to take a Sabbath rest, we are not being humble people. Instead, we become people who are wrapped up in ourselves and our self-centered world. Out of touch with God, we become fearful of death, evil, God's discipline, The Lord's table, and His house. We grow dangerously close to the fall pride has prepared for us. Can we stop the deterioration and return to the fold? A key to living the humble life is rest. Be humble and rest.

Get Spiritual Quick

One day, lacking direction for my writing, I decided to blindly open my Bible, stick my finger in and hope to land on a verse about humility. On my first attempt I touched verse thirty-seven, chapter nineteen of Acts. *"For you have brought these men here who are neither robbers of temples nor blasphemers of our goddess."* This was said by the town clerk at Ephesus to a confused crowd which had been stirred up by the city silversmiths. If there was something there about humility, I wasn't seeing it. So, I turned a few pages hoping to find the Gospels and struck with my finger again. This time I found Luke sixteen, verse two. *"And he called him and said to him, 'What is this I hear about you? Give an accounting of your management, for you can no longer be manager.'"* Aha! The story of the unrighteous steward, a man humiliated by his own incompetence. I suppose there is a lesson about humility there somewhere, but I was too lazy to search for it. I continued my search. After a couple more flip and flop attempts at receiving accidental inspiration, I decided that there was something prideful and lacking of humility when expecting God to respond to my impersonal, shooting-in-the-dark and rolling-the-dice style of studying.

Seeking a word from God requires a humble approach to devotion and not a dart board with random verses pinned to it. Our get-spiritual-quick methods resemble our get-rich-quick plans. Pick the winning numbers, and our spiritual poverty is immediately erased. Send in your entry form, making sure you transfer the gold seal from your prize ticket to your enclosed reply envelope and you MAY already have won a deeper understanding of scripture, faith that can move mountains, and the cattle on a thousand hills (or is it sheep?).

Inspiration doesn't come that way, nor does spiritual growth. Rather, inspiration, communication, revelation, and maturation are products of a commitment to a personal love relationship with the lover of our souls. Loving God requires more than showing up for church every Easter and more than saying the same prayer five times per day. We must stop attempting selfish shortcuts and give God some daily time, undivided attention, and sincere adoration. An attitude of humility provides a willingness to wait upon God for direction and inspiration, with anticipation and an ever-increasing awareness of His presence, while traveling a disciplined path of Bible study, prayer, and devotion. Humble yourself!

Charlotte's Web[24]

The story of Charlotte's Web offers a little surprise when Charlotte's third wonder web appears at the end. I must admit I never read the story of the runty pig destined for Christmas dinner but later saved by animals and a spider in Zuckerman's barn. I saw the movie. Charlotte the spider was quite resourceful as she sought to save the pig by increasing the young pig's perceived value with a specially spun web word. Her first message appearing in the morning light revealed the words *SOME PIG* to the delight of family and neighbors. Who could argue with such a miraculous message? In need of further accolades to prevent the piggy's demise, Charlotte spun another web with the word *TERRIFIC*.

Since the web was strung at the top of the barn door, one wonders why it is assumed that the words were meant to describe the pig and not the goose, ewe, horse or the web weaving spider. Nevertheless, ole Zuckerman decided this swine was so special he would enter him in the fair. Most of us know, even without actual farm experience, that the pig that gets the blue ribbon at the county fair is usually the hog that is so big it earns the right to be called a hog. This little pig named Wilbur would never be more than a scrawny pig, but this pig-headed family thought two heavenly-sent spider webs were enough to render a pig worth more than his weight.

Their expectation increased when another web appeared in Wilbur's stall at the fair with a word that would surely convince any judge that Wilbur was a prize pig. No porker's rolls of fat and scale-busting obesity could beat this piglet's personality. If there was ever an undersized hog that should be given the top-oinker award, it was Wilbur because he was, as Charlotte's web

---

[24] E.B.White, *Charlotte's Web* (Harper Collins, 1952).

proclaimed, *HUMBLE*. The truth is, as I see it, we are more likely to win the world's trophies if we can convince everyone we are *SOME PIG* or *TERRIFIC* than if they recognize us as *HUMBLE*. Wilbur didn't win the blue-ribbon. He did, however, win the love and appreciation of his family and friends. Humility doesn't win many contests, but it does make us special. In fact, it makes us special to God. Maybe the story of Wilbur asks an important life question. Who do we aspire to be? Hog or Humble?

Humility That Conquers

Humility is a great trait but is worthless apart from the power and presence of the Lord in our lives. From his book *Humility*, Andrew Murray makes what I believe is a questionable assertion.

"Until a humility which will rest in nothing less than the end and death of self; which gives up all the honor of men as Jesus did, to seek the honor that comes from God alone; which absolutely makes and counts itself nothing, that God may be all, that the Lord alone may be exalted, until such a humility be what we seek in Christ above our chief joy, and welcome at any price, there is very little hope of a religion that will conquer the world."[25]

Well then, there is very little hope indeed. If to conquer the world, Christianity is dependent upon Christians achieving the kind of humility to which we are all called, which exalts Christ alone, and dies daily to self; then Christianity is destined to failure. I only hope that Christians will desire and aspire to that kind of humility. I little expect that believers will actually achieve it

---

[25] Andrew Murray, *Humility* (Gainesville, FL: Bridge-Logos, 2000), 10,11.

day to day, month to month, etc. Being humble is a constant struggle. Pride is a monster always lurking in the shadows. Humility is a choice to be made as often as the stream of life has ripples, or the road of life has rocks.

I am glad that God is not waiting to conquer the world until we learn to be humble. We can rest assured that God will do that without us. Jesus never asks, "Are you humble?" He does, however ask, *"Do you now believe?"* He followed that question in John 19 verse 33 with these words. *"In the world you have tribulation, but take courage; I have overcome the world."*

The Apostle John assures us that in Christ we ARE overcomers. *"For whatever is born of God overcomes the world; and this is the victory that has overcome the world - our faith. Who is the one who overcomes the world, but he who believes that Jesus is the Son of God?"* (1 John 5:4-5)

There are people today who seek to overcome the world with their brand of religion, relying upon disciples who have achieved a high level of humility in which they have pledged to totally sacrifice self in order that their lord may be exalted, and their god may be honored. Our humility may never match theirs. That is why we must be very clear. The only humility that will ever be the instrument by which the world is overcome is that of Jesus who offered Himself as a sacrifice for sin in obedience to the will of the Father. A time will come when non-believers will seem to have overcome by their submission and selflessness. Revelation 17:12 to 14 tells us,

> *"And the ten horns which you saw are ten kings, who have not yet received a kingdom, but they receive authority as kings with the beast for one hour. These have one purpose and they give their power and authority to the beast. These will wage war against the Lamb, and the Lamb will overcome them, because He is Lord of lords and King of*

kings, and those who are with Him are the called and chosen and faithful."

I just want to set the record straight. We choose to be humble because it is the character of our Lord. We are learning to desire humility as we mature in our faith. We are not seeking to be selfless out of some false belief that God's power to accomplish His will is dependent upon a *"humility which will rest in nothing less than the end and death of self"* (from Andrew Murray). We have overcome the world because *"greater is He who is in you, than He who is in the world"* (1 John 4:4). Our humility, like our righteousness, is *"like a filthy garment"* (Isaiah 64:6).

The True Way To Be Humble

Phillips Brooks is the author of the familiar Christmas hymn "O Little Town of Bethlehem." In that song we are reminded, "In this world of sin, where meek souls will receive Him, still the dear Christ enters in."[26] Brooks is known for another word about humility. Consider one of his popular quotes. "The true way to be humble is not to stoop until you are smaller than yourself, but to stand at your real height against some higher nature that will show you what the real smallness of your greatness is."[27] Let's take his words and visualize the idea, coupled with the lines of the 100th Psalm. If we use a little imagination we

---

[26] Phillips Brooks, "O Little Town of Bethlehem," *The Baptist Hymnal* (Nashville: Convention Press, 1991), 86

[27] Brainyquote.com/quotes/Phillips_brooks_121609

can demonstrate bold humility in the psalmist's celebration of the greatness of God.

> 1 Stand up. Stand tall and *"shout joyfully to the Lord, all the earth."*
> 2 With strong arms and fearless labor *"serve the Lord with gladness."*
> With great leaping strides run swiftly as the Almighty invites us to *"come before Him with joyful singing."*
> 3 We may have some authority, power and greatness but we also *"know that the Lord Himself is God."* We have accomplishments and achievements and confess *"It is He who has made us, and not we ourselves."* Conscious of people and things in our personal sphere of influence, we herald *"we are His people and the sheep of His pasture."*
> 4 In the midst of our busyness to work and play, we will periodically pause to *"enter His gates with thanksgiving and His courts with praise."* We will without ceasing *"Give thanks to Him,"* and *"bless His name."*
> 5 Though our character compared to that of others may be commendable, we boldly declare that *"the Lord is good; His loving-kindness is everlasting and His faithfulness to all generations."*

God has given us great opportunities to achieve, possess, and conquer. He expects us to be resourceful with all He gives to us (Parable of the Talents, Mathew 25:14-30). Humble praise does not involve hiding who we are. It is boldly standing before God as a personal testimony of who He is. Though we stand on top of a mountain of personal trophies, academic degrees, letters of commendation, bank accounts, titles, merits and medals, on our toes with neck and back stretched to their limit in order to claim as much stature as possible, we still will never reach God's hand without His reaching down for ours. With chest expanded and our tail feathers spread revealing all our glory, we are but a turkey standing next to a phoenix. King David in royal robe and crown, looking from his palace at the kingdom over which he ruled, was wise to see beyond himself. Psalm 104 is another of the great praise passages from his pen.

> *"Bless the Lord, O my soul! O Lord my God, You are very great; You are clothed with splendor and majesty, covering Yourself with light as with a cloak, Stretching out heaven like a tent curtain. He lays the beams of His upper chambers in the waters; He makes the clouds His chariot; He walks upon the wings of the wind; He makes the winds His messengers, Flaming fire His ministers."*
> *(Psalm 104:1-4)*

How can we stand before Him and not be humble? How can we come boldly before Him and not assume a humble position? How can we live life granted us by our awesome God and not choose to walk humbly every day with Him? Come on! Get humble!

CHAPTER EIGHT

CHOOSING HUMILITY

"To sum up, all of you be harmonious, sympathetic, brotherly, kindhearted, and humble in spirit; not returning evil for evil or insult for insult, but giving a blessing instead; for you were called for the very purpose that you might inherit a blessing."
1 Peter 3:8-9

☙❧

What is the best and most important virtue for living the Christian life? Many Christians would say love is. Others would answer, Faith! Still others might believe it is always asking the question, "What would Jesus do?" (I realize that is not a virtue, but hey!) Humility may not be the virtue anyone will answer. It is a quality not many Christians claim or covet. Augustine, a fourth century philosopher and Catholic theologian, said, "Should you ask me: What is the first thing in religion? I should reply: the first, second, and third thing therein is humility."[28] An essential element for Christ-like living is humility. It is a valuable virtue in the exercise of our love, faith, and dedication to doing what Jesus would do.

Love without the presence of humility may simply be self-love or lust. Being loved is more pleasurable when it comes to us humbly. It is more believable also. If love is the deep desire

---

[28] Robert J. Morgan, *Nelson's Complete Book of Stories, Illustrations, & Quotes* (Nashville: Thomas Nelson, Inc., 2000), 456.

for someone else's best without regard for one's own self, then that unselfish devotion must be guided by a humble heart. True love and humility are complementary. Each improves the other.

Our faith with the absence of humility may be more selfish dependence than confident trust. The attitude of humility looks to the object of our faith with selfless devotion. With all conceit and self-reliance set aside, we can unencumbered clutch the hand of God. Self-centered pride trusts for the purpose of receiving some personal gratification. Selfless humility acts on faith with fearless disregard for personal gain or loss.

The question, "What would Jesus do?", may contain spiritually devastating pious pride if answers are not governed by humility. Why do we ask the question? Are we *"sounding a trumpet before you, as the hypocrites do in the synagogues and in the streets, so that they may be honored by men?"* (Matthew 6:2). Or, are we humbly interested in emulating the Lord of our life? Humility makes a difference. Which will be our choice? Humility? Pride? Let's choose to be humble.

Ugly Powerless Losers

There are reasons why some people have a high self-esteem and others a low self-esteem. It is somewhat natural for the very attractive person to have a higher self-esteem than the person who is very unattractive. We would expect the person who has been successful in his or her profession to have a higher regard for themselves than the individual who has failed to succeed. Someone sitting in the boss's chair will inevitably hold herself with greater respect that the one who must bring her a cup of coffee. Which group will have the easiest time achieving true humility? Those with low self-esteem or high self-esteem? Our obvious choice is those who are ugly, powerless losers. Humility should be easy for them. If it is easier for them, it is still not easy. Low self-esteem should not be mistaken for humility. There are many people who moan and groan over their unfortunate lot in life, who readily admit to being undesirable, disadvantaged, inadequate and impotent, but are far from truly humble. True humility may be as big a stretch for them as it is for the good-looking, highly successful, dominant ones. A person probably does not exist for whom authentic humility is inherent or intrinsic.

For everyone and anyone humility is a hard choice. It is behavior which we must learn to value and then adopt as a personal characteristic like we would honesty, integrity, or mercy. It is a muscle which must be exercised. While assessing our strengths or lack of strengths, we each must decide how to discipline ourselves in the behaviors we deem important. In our daily walk, as we gloat or groan, boast or bewail, crow or cry, shout or spit, can we receive whatever is our fortune or mis-fortune with a great big dose of humility? Humble living will always be God's desire and our challenge to accept. None of us can claim total responsibility for the condition of the road upon which we travel. We can, however, determine to travel that road with a humility that will be pleasing to other travelers and will please the one who determines where that road ends.

Credit Conscious Leaders

Giving credit to those who deserve it and seeking no credit for one's own work are two facets of humility. The humble person understands this. Humility does not want to take credit for something someone else did, nor is it interested in receiving credit for its own commendable deeds. Humble people enjoy turning the spotlight on others and holding up the applaud sign. It is most virtuous when good reasons to be prideful are dismissed in favor of humility.

What an aid to leadership humility is! It is a character strength which renders leaders more effective. Employees and subordinates are far more loyal and productive when management generously doles out due credit. A leader is equally more follow-able when he or she demonstrates an aversion to self-praise and self-recognition. That attitude wins leaders far more admiration than the attitude of self-promotion.

Humility is a quality which frees leaders to be dynamic leaders. A Greek scholar named Benjamin Jowett is credited with saying, "The way to get things done is not to mind who gets the credit for doing them."[29] I have known leaders who were so worried with getting credit for their great accomplishments that other opportunities passed by them unnoticed and not seized. Life's journey moves along too swiftly to pause and gloat. Arrogance limits vision. Humble leaders are able to keep eyes fixed on new things ahead, because they do not stop to listen to applause, bow to the audience, and revel in what has past. Credit consuming pride has felled many leaders. Humility will propel leaders to heights only attainable to the humble.

Uncommon Virtue

In a small child it is sweet, but humility in one who is powerful with every reason to be prideful but chooses to be humble is the stuff of admiration. Admittedly, since finding humility in

---

[29] https://www.goodreads.com/author/quotes/13395658.Benjamin_Jowett

children can be rare moments, those are precious and wonderful moments also. The child's humility emerges from the awareness of his/her own helplessness and total dependence upon others. Adults live in a world which they may imagine to be of their own making. Persons who are smart, hard workers, make good decisions along the way, and live disciplined lives, may consider humility unnecessary. They may think it more appropriate adorning those who have suffered from ignorance, laziness, poor decisions and undisciplined living. They will miss the joy that humility adds to success.

Successful adults who admit their vulnerability and dependence on others will find humility a comfortable attire. With honest reflection upon the process of our achievements, we should be aware that other people make possible our successes. Parents, grandparents, friends, teachers, co-workers, supervisors, political leaders, self-sacrificing men and women in uniform, business executives, entrepreneurs, farmers, doctors, etc., make good things in our lives possible. In addition to honest reflection, spiritual eyesight will enable us to acknowledge that without God's care, control, compassion, and constant contribution to our cause we will have no success at all. Even with honest reflection and mature spiritual insight, humility is a choice. When it is not forced upon us and comes by our own choosing, it is indeed admirable. It is commendable because, although it should be understood as the best choice, it is a choice few choose.

Teaching Children Humility

If what they are saying about humility is true (and I believe it is) parents need to spend as much time teaching humility as they spend providing correction. The following quote is from a book called *Parenting is Heart Work* by Doctor Turansky and Nurse Joanne Miller. "Humility is a heart issue and an essential ingredient in our lives. In fact, the greater the humility, the more a person can benefit from correction."[30] Teaching humility is a little like preparing the soil before scattering seeds. If we don't take the time to improve the soil before planting seeds, our later labor to extricate weeds may be an endless effort producing disappointing results. The soil is dependent upon our care, provision of nourishment, protection from harmful outside influences, removal of impurities, observation of good and bad indicators, and securing professionals to assist with our God given responsibilities. If the soil resists our efforts, then all of that correcting becomes tougher and perhaps fruitless. Some soil is tougher to make fertile than other soil.

Of course, we are talking about children. We can't teach soil to be humble, but we can teach it to children. All our responsibilities of nurturing and training our children will be easier if the children can experience good examples of humility and learn to be humble. Turansky and Miller have provided a valuable principle in child-rearing. "The greater the humility, the more a person can benefit from correction."

Many parents know the pain of living with a child that will not accept direction, correction, instruction, or even affection. The home must become a place where mom and dad humbly serve each other, expose a heart of humility before their children, and model a humble devotion to Christ and His church. Humility must be practiced in all our communication, recreation, occupation, and avocation. It is the first course of a four-course meal. Children should witness a humble offering of thanks before each meal, a humble prayer over them as we send

---

[30] Dr.Scott Teransky and Joanne Miller, *Parenting is Heart Work* (Colorado Springs, CO: David C Cook, 2005)

them off to school, and humble intercessory prayer as we tuck them into bed. The children may not at first be able to name the atmosphere of their home, but they will breathe in the air of humility and will learn to enjoy it, appreciate it, and thrive in it. Correction will always be the parents' responsibility, but that correction will be all the more beneficial if we have first prepared our children to humbly receive it. Children will probably not be more humble than their parents. So, we can only hope that parents will choose to live the humble life.

Names for Children

Sometimes we name our children after personal characteristics or things which we admire and desire. Here are a few examples. We name sons Hunter, Champ, Christian, Max, Prince, Rich, Rock, or Victor. Girl names are the best examples of meaningful character. They are named Angel, Candy, Faith, Grace, Hope, Patience, Prudence, and Serenity. It would be great if we thought so highly of humility that we named our children after it. Girls might be named Humblina, Lowla, Humilla, or Momique (more meek). We could name a son Kneel, Hum Bo, Less, or Dennye (Deny). The fact is, humility doesn't occupy a very high place in our hierarchy of Holy behavior. When perusing warm, sweet, meaningful names for our children, humility isn't a word that comes to mind. Probably no new mom and dad have ever had a conversation about how they could create a novel new name that represents the virtue humility. We like making up new names, don't we? We name children after cars, fads, businesses, new technological inventions, and fictional characters. I wonder if anyone has already named a child Apple, Meta, Pixel, or Vector. When we consider all the ridiculous names which have been stuck on a child, the name Humility doesn't sound all that bad, does it? Perhaps we could make popular this new phrase, "Be it ever so holy, there's no name like humble."

Boasting About Tomorrow

There is something to be learned about choosing humility from occasions when circumstances humble us without our choosing. I have often said that being made humble does not count for character. When our pride gets knocked down by some extremely stupid and embarrassing mistake, or when we get cut off at the knees by someone who far excels in something with which we were prideful, we are humbled. We did not choose in these instances to be humble. We merely suffered a loss of pride. When our reasons for pride are taken away by an economic crisis that guts our investment portfolio, or a company crisis that results in our demotion or loss of job, then we are made humble. We have not chosen humility with a desire to be virtuous. Humble has chosen us.

Maybe in these humbling experiences, we can learn about humility so that later we prefer it. One lesson we might learn is how few things we can take total credit for and how little control over life's circumstances we actually have. The athlete who excels today may tomorrow be a paraplegic. The business owner today could tomorrow be the janitor. The bountiful crops today could tomorrow suffer drought. The mansion today could tomorrow be in ashes. The great nation today could tomorrow fall apart. That all sounds pretty pessimistic. The point is, whatever we enjoy today should be counted as a blessing, not cause for boasting. *"Do not boast about tomorrow, for you do not know what a day may bring forth"* (Proverbs 27:1).

Allow me to repeat a Bible verse which is repeated throughout this book. From the New Testament book of James comes this instruction, *"Humble yourselves in the presence of the Lord, and He will exalt you"* (James 4:10). Immediately after this, James gives us this council:

> *"Come now, you who say, 'today or tomorrow we will go to such and such a city, and spend a year there and engage in business and make a profit.' Yet you do not know what your life will be like tomorrow. You are just a vapor that appears for a little while and then vanishes away. Instead you ought to say, 'If the Lord wills, we will live and also do this or that.' But as it is, you boast in your arrogance; all such boasting is evil." (James 4:13-16)*

No matter our circumstances, whether rich or poor, powerful or weak, smooth sailing or ship-wrecked, we must choose to be humble. *"But may it never be,"* says Paul, *"that I would boast, except in the cross of our Lord Jesus Christ . . ."* (Galatians 6:14). When occasions for boasting come, choose humility instead.

Self-Serving Humility

While there are many benefits for practicing humility, we must choose to be humble because it is right, not because it makes us look good. Knowing that humility is an appealing quality, some masquerade humility to win favor. They find that when they act humbly, they can manipulate others to do what they want. Humility becomes a disguise to hide true intentions. This self-serving false humility is so prevalent that we find ourselves suspicious of people who act humbly. Another misuse of humility is when it is employed to win forgiveness. It is much easier to forgive someone who is contrite and lowly. How can we know if they are truly humble or just faking it for the sympathy? Both the criminal and the con have learned how to resemble humility when appealing for pardon or convincing a victim. Even if the humility is real, a truly humble person should not use that quality to escape consequences for their actions or for dishonest gain.

Virtue should give rise to other virtue. In Peter's second letter he says, *". . . in your faith supply moral excellence, and in your moral excellence, knowledge, and in your knowledge, self-control, and in your self-control, perseverance, and in your perseverance, godliness, and in your godliness, brotherly kindness, and in your brotherly kindness, love"* (2 Peter 1:5-7). Humility should be a byway to the highway, not a visa to vanity.

One other way humility is wrongfully applied is when we attempt to virtuously accept premature defeat. There is no virtue in surrender and no humility in mediocrity. Humiliation is not humility. The loser's attempt at humility is not applaudable. It is the humble winner that inspires us and demonstrates commendable humility. Isn't it interesting that the selfish person would incorporate a quality of servility and selflessness to advance their selfish purposes? Those who are self-centered will never know the fulfillment found along the path of **true humility**.

MacArthur's Prayer

Prayer is essential to the humble life for so many reasons. It is both an act of humility and a conduit through which God awakens humility in us. We humble ourselves to pray, and then pray for God to keep us humble. The more we humble ourselves and gain humility, the more we find ourselves praying for the needs of others. Out of our concern for others and awareness of the destructive nature of pride, we humbly pray that others will also choose to be humble.

General MacArthur is given credit for this prayer called *Father's Prayer*.[31]

"Build me a son, O God, who will be strong enough to know when he is weak and brave enough to face himself when he is afraid; one who will be proud and unbending in defeat, but humble and gentle in victory. . . . Build me a son whose heart will be clear, whose goal will be high; a son who will master himself before he seeks to master others; one who will learn to laugh, yet never forget how to weep; one who will reach into the future, yet never forget the past, and after all these things are his, this I pray, enough sense of humor that he may always be serious yet never take himself too seriously."

His prayer recognizes the high place of humility, and MacArthur finishes the prayer for his son with this:

"Give him humility so that he may always remember the simplicity of true greatness, the open mind of true wisdom, the meekness of true strength; then I, his father, will dare to whisper, 'I have not lived in vain.'"

Oh, that we were all noble enough to believe in the value of humility so much that we would practice it daily, and petition

---

[31] Alice Gray, comp., *Stories for the Heart* (Sisters, Oregon: Multnomah Books, 1996), 193.

God for His work in the lives of our children to include the development of a character that cherishes the humble life.

Uncharacteristic Humility

A lot of pride-swallowing humility may be necessary to show up for an apology session after on-the-job misconduct, but it all may appear to fellow employees like job-saving humility if they have not seen any humility in us before. (Please read that long sentence once more and slowly.) Showing humility after an episode of completely losing control of temper and tongue may be the best direction, but don't be surprised if to others we are not believably humble. Some people have lived such that they would have to undergo a change of character for a long, long time before any attempt at humility would be credible. The point is, how uncharacteristic is humility for us?

Even non-Christians expect to find this virtue in Christians. They are familiar enough with the Bible and the teachings of Jesus to know that humility should be evident in followers of Christ. Our goal should be to make humility the norm for us (no pun intended). Humility could become commonly expected if it is our normal go-to response. If people find that we are most often humble, then when we do something that requires a humble apology, our humility is less likely to be questioned. It is difficult to reject an apology from someone who is characteristically humble. Imagine trying to hold a grudge after a confession from the Pope or apology from Billy Graham. I would list some others, but it is difficult to come up with names of people who have a reputation of being humble.

How many of our names come to the minds of others when they look for an example of humility to follow? How many people will understand better what the biblical call to humility is by watching us? Humility must never become a trait we turn on only when there is need to gain personal favor or approval. Those who are truly humble put on humility every day before they walk out the door. Humility is not the suit we wear only to special occasions. It is everyday clothing. It is a valuable trait tried and tested through time by those who love to live the humble life.

Thorns and Humility

God blesses us far beyond what we ask or think. His abundant blessings absolutely amaze us. From the hand of God comes provision, protection, power, and purpose. There are times when we receive God's good and are tempted to claim responsibility for receiving the good. God blessed me because I am obedient, or because I made right decisions, or because I became committed to Jesus early in life. It is easy to get puffed up. Humility fades and sinful pride swells. Pride places us in position to receive the disciplining hand of God. For His correction we should give thanks. By it, we are kept from remaining prideful. It isn't easy to remain humble. God helps us.

Paul told us in 2 Corinthians 12:7, *". . . to keep me from exalting myself, there was given me a thorn in the flesh."* Rather than prickly speculation on what that *"thorn in the flesh"* was, we need to care what its purpose was. If we will receive it, *"a thorn in the flesh"* that keeps us humble is much preferred to the employment of God's harsher discipline. Do we ever thank God for the person He used in our life to keep us humble? Have we ever thanked God for that physical disfigurement that He used to maintain our humility? Have we ever thanked God for that event which brought us to our knees before Him? Don't let a blessing of God become a source of sinful pride. Also, don't let the "thorn in the flesh" be received with ingratitude. If you dare, pray this prayer: "Lord, keep us humble."

Humility Teacher

Humility is not something you easily teach. Just when you think you understand it, God gives you an opportunity to learn something new. Kicking back pride and letting go of self is an exhilarating battle. Great enjoyment comes when we successfully concentrate on others and stop putting self first or second or next. Accomplishing something worthwhile without caring who gets the credit is liberating. Watching someone else take credit for something you did without being overcome with resentment, bitterness, or a need to defend yourself, brings on a reassuring inner strength and calm.

Humility – it does a body good. But watch out! Just when we think we can help someone else understand humility, God reveals a big wad of pride hidden away in a dark corner of our skull. When we first see it, we aren't sure what we are looking at. Then, we try to deny it. Then, we get a nauseating feeling like we're going to hurl any minute. We thought we had swept the house clean. No more pride. But there it is - dark, ugly, and stinky. If we could just throw it out, forget it, and pretend it wasn't ours, we could return to enjoying our humility.

What good is humility if pride is still present? Maybe it is very good. Maybe discovering a new pocket of pride helps us teach its hideousness and insidiousness. We learn that we can't let our guard down. There is always new opportunity to resist pride and exercise the faith, love, and compassion that keeps pride from winning. We can introduce other people to humility, with humble encouragement as a watchful warrior. The teacher of humility can not take pride in helping someone else find humility any more than she can take pride in her own inner struggle for it. We must keep reminding ourselves that humble begins as one who has forgotten the words. Hummmm. Know what I mean?

The best way to teach humility is to be an example of it. We can be identifiably humble so that people wanting to learn about humility can see what it looks like. If not you or me, who? Who else is able to lead others to choose the humble life? There are lots of examples of vanity, selfishness, conceit, and narcissism. The only way many people can understand humility is by rejecting behavior that proceeds from pride. They can easily see what humility isn't. The only way they may see truly honorable humility is when they encounter it in us.

Christian Weirdo

Are we ever embarrassed about being identified as a Christian when we try to mix in with a non-Christian crowd? Awkward moments are best handled with humility, but Christians often let pride surface and get us in trouble. Attempting to cover up embarrassment, pride produces behavior that is contrary to our Christian principles. Non-believers characterize Christians as weirdoes if we carry a Bible, are uninterested in alcohol, avoid wild parties, are virgins, demonstrate a humble spirit, or say anything about a holy lifestyle. In order to show we are just as cool as they are, we loosen our standards and blend in. Things are said and done that we will ask God's forgiveness for later, but for the moment our pride is allowed to dictate our actions.

True humility isn't pushed around so easily. Humble Christians aren't so worried about how we may be portrayed by unbelievers or even by fellow believers. The urge to defend ourselves or the desire to gain the wrong crowd's approval isn't the reaction of humility. Humility is able to duck beneath the critic's punch. Pride, standing tall, provides a bigger target which usually results in a disappointing performance. It is curious how pride is understood as strength while humility is looked upon as weakness. In challenging, embarrassing, and even threatening moments, it is humble Christians who come out on top and the prideful ones who fail and fall. Humility enables Christians to endure disapproval, underwhelm the critic, and continue to be the weirdo, goody-goody, religious wacko Christians we are proud to be. Or something like that.

Humility and Joy

Rejoicing when good happens and good things come is best when exuding from a humble spirit rather than exploding from a prideful one. Humility is allowed to celebrate. It does not have to suppress exuberance. Failing to take delight in achievement, endowment, fulfillment, and amusement is to practice some form of stoicism or cynicism rather than Christianity. Christians know joy, and they know how to be joyful. Humble joy is not dependent upon material things or temporal pleasures, but it does not reject them either. We believe that *"all good things come from above."* When good things happen or we get good things, we give God thanks. Rejoicing is an expression of gratitude. There is a recognizable difference between prideful gloating over good gotten, and the humble gladness over what has been given. It is possible to be full of joy without being pumped up with pride. Limited laughter and hesitant happiness is not the face of humility. The humble person will find that humility continues to be evident in moments of ecstatic joy. Rejoice without shame or apology. Remember in the naming of spiritual fruit in Galatians, the second in that list is *JOY*. *"But the fruit of the Spirit is love, joy, peace, patience, kindness, goodness, faithfulness, gentleness, self-control. Against such things there is no law"* (Galatians 5:22-23).

Stinkin' Thinkin'

Self-talk can encourage humble living or discombobulate it. You know, like the things we say to ourselves when someone hurts us or when they disrespect us. Thoughts that pop into our heads when we feel we have been wronged generate either kind words whispered from a humble spirit or mean words muttered from pride. Consider this example: A teenager in a big, white, Toyota pickup fails to yield as we are walking across from the parking lot to a store. Do we say angrily to ourselves, "These teenage drivers are reckless and irresponsible," or do we compassionately say to ourselves, "That poor teenager. No one ever loved him enough to teach him manners"?

How about this? An elderly lady takes our order at Wendy's. After she finally finds the correct buttons on the register, our order is handed to us with the wrong sandwich and no fries. Do we mumble, "This stupid, stupid, woman! What does Grandma think she is doing?" Or, is our self-talk more like this? "I'm so proud that old woman is trying to be active and productive."

Here is one more example: The phone rings, and when I answer it, a recording begins immediately with a message from a local politician. After slamming down our phone, we think to ourselves, "Why would this idiot think I would vote for someone who rudely interrupted 'The Walking Dead'?" Or do we have more humble thoughts like, "How nice it is to know our politicians can afford a high-tech mass calling system"?

The point is this. Words that we think during those aggravating situations are as telling about our humility as other actions and spoken words. Learning to temper our thoughts and soften our self-talk can make all the more probable our humble manner and demeanor. Humility requires work. That work begins at the very moment we are messed with. Lose the battle there, and the battle gets tougher. Watch out for stinkin' thinkin'. It is an enemy of **true humility**.

Humility and The Elderly

Every stage of life is best when entered with some humility. It is particularly interesting to observe elder citizens who let their pride make them angry in their old age. Pride causes a senior adult to resent youthful persons around them, to get offended when assistance is offered, to get irritated quickly when mistakes are made, to get frustrated when new technology surpasses them, to fume and spit when they think someone is showing disrespect, and to fiercely defend their way of doing anything that is now being done differently. It is pride that causes the pot to boil over. It is pride that produces the raging storm that drives people away and makes life more lonely than ever. Fear, insecurity, and loss are blamed, but pride is the agitator.

Pride is the poison that gets under our skin and drives us mad. It speeds up the deterioration of life. Humility is a healer and preserver of life. When the elderly face aging with humility, they are empowered by their years rather than overwhelmed by them. Frustrations and irritations, even fear and loss, lose some of their sting when we are humble. Self-imposed pressures are released by humility, making life easier to enjoy. Humility doesn't do away with the challenges of old age. Humility does allow the elderly to face real challenges without creating artificial and unnecessary ones. The challenge for younger folk is to help the older folk to see pride as their enemy. Unfortunately, pride will not allow the old folks to be convinced of anything by young folks. Maybe young people will remember when they grow old what they have seen pride do to old people. If we choose to learn humility while we are young, then when age finally catches up with us, we may be able to enter into those final years with more joy.

There are so many reasons for choosing to be humble. Young and old, rich and poor, healthy and sick, working and jobless, powerful and powerless, are all people who will fare better by choosing a life of humility.

Don't Help Me!

Why is accepting a helping hand so hard? "I don't want any help. Leave me alone. I can do it myself." This isn't always our reaction. With some tasks we gladly accept aid. With other tasks the offer of help seems to imply we are incapable or insufficient. Still other tasks make us feel like we are being robbed of womanhood or manhood when someone steps in to help, especially when that helper is the opposite sex. Resistance to accept assistance may reveal many things about us. One thing it shows is the presence of sinful pride. Are we too proud to accept directions, financial assistance, encouragement, a different idea, a cup of tea, or a small suggestion? Are we too proud to share our work with someone else? Are we too proud to be vulnerable or dependent? Reluctance to receive help from others shows distaste for humility or at least a lack of appreciation for this biblically mandated virtue. Humility is the cure for the negative feelings which arise when help is offered. It is a pathway toward conquering the anger, resentment, lowered self-worth, anxiety, and frustration that surfaces whenever someone tries to be helpful.

Our dislike for assistance also pops up in our relationship with God. We readily ask God for many things, but there are other things about which we avoid asking. Perhaps we don't want to feel we are completely dependent upon God. There are some things we can do ourselves. Right? We love trusting God for some provision and some protection, but reserve some segments of our life to trust only ourselves. Like fixing people. That's one activity I must take care of. I can't trust God with that. I have to do it. God could probably fix them, but not the way I would.

Pride keeps us from totally letting go and letting God. Why? Why is it difficult to *"Trust in the Lord with all your heart and do not lean on your own understanding?"* Why can't we fully follow these wise words? *"In all your ways acknowledge Him, and He will make your paths straight. Do not be wise in your own eyes; fear the Lord and turn away from evil. It will be healing to your body and refreshment to your bones"* (Proverbs 3:5-8). Until we can completely lean upon God, we have not learned to love humility. Until we have learned to be humble, we cannot completely love and trust God.

Life's Bumpy Road

We all travel down the rugged roadway of life finding humbling moments thrust upon us at various intersections. Marriage begins and ends with humility. The male gets down on his knees and humbly asks his sweetheart to become his bride. The politician begins public service with a humble ceremony promising truth with one hand on the Bible, followed by great promises made out of the other side of his or her mouth. Years of required education force us to sit in uncomfortable desks while humbly allowing a teacher to force feed us facts.

The Christian life begins with the very humble act of baptism. The new convert, robed and barefoot, submits to being lowered into the water and then rises to stand before an audience of believers with hair a mess, makeup running, and bubbles sputtering from mouth and nose. It is an appropriately humble experience. Appropriate because it comes after the equally humble act of confessing sin, repenting of sin, and receiving forgiveness.

If we really want to learn humility, we can go to the hospital for surgery. We undress, put on a robe that will not cover our rear, put our teeth in a bed side bowl, take off all our jewelry, lie down on a bed that will be wheeled down the hall past gawking strangers, ride into an elevator where someone will ask, "going to surgery?", wind up in a cold post-op room for an hour, and then try to get someone's attention to tell them we need to go potty - quite the humbling event.

If we value humility, we will not be intimidated by life's humbling situations. If we cannot swallow pride and take on a lowly spirit, we can expect the rough places in the road of life will be unbearable. The humble life really is the more practical approach. Life's mean moments will reveal that humility is strength, and pride is weakness. The humble are able to bow and bend without breaking. Those full of pride are the more likely to snap when pressured to lower themselves, and they cannot. The sooner we choose to be humble, the sooner we are able to accept that stature, high position, and pride do not exempt us from common ruts and potholes. When we choose to be humble, we are able to get past the desire to spew and fuss about bumpy roads - and move on.

Not My Will, But Thine

God gives us opportunities to stand humbly before Him and say, *"nevertheless, not my will, but thine be done"* (Luke 22:42). Our proper position before God is humility. He provides for the exercise of that humility. Our experiences are not for God's benefit but for ours. Humility causes us to shut our mouths so that we can hear His voice. It helps us let go of things so that we can love Him. It draws our eyes away from the world so that we can see His work. It allows us to open our hands and hearts to receive His blessings. The opportunities that God provides for us to be humble are almost never moments for which we have asked. Moses never asked to become a deliverer. Job never asked for his troubles. Jonah didn't ask to be a preacher. David didn't ask for the great responsibility of being king. Jeremiah didn't ask to be a prophet. Daniel didn't ask to be led away in captivity. The persons whom Jesus healed to give evidence of His Messiahship didn't ask to be blind, crippled, sick, or dead. Jesus did not even ask the Father for the privilege of suffering for our sin. It was the Father's will.

God has the authority to change the course of our lives at whatever moment He chooses. Many of the paths upon which we are placed are intended to produce within us humility that will lead to great adventures in the power and presence of God. A debilitating illness, life-changing handicap, death of a loved one, loss of employment, call into ministry, job promotion, election to public office, natural disaster, personal attack by someone with power to do great harm, inheritance of great wealth, early retirement, or discovering a new friend, all may hold equal opportunities for us to bend the knee and bow the head before almighty God and humbly declare, *"Nevertheless, not my will, but Thine be done."* What a rush of joy, excitement, and enthusiasm can be had when we can boldly face any occasion with expectations of a new journey ahead; a journey in which the view is always more brilliant and rich when we choose to be humble.

CHAPTER NINE

OUR HUMBLE GOD

Blessed be the God and Father of our Lord Jesus Christ, the Father of mercies and God of all comfort, who comforts us in all our affliction so that we will be able to comfort those who are in any affliction with the comfort with which we ourselves are comforted by God.
2 Corinthians 1:3-4

ೲ

It is difficult imagining God as humble because we know Him as our almighty and exalted God and ourselves as lowly man. Of course, our inability to see God as humble is due to our continued misunderstanding of humility. We think humility is a requirement for us so that we accept the authority of our Heavenly Father and our responsibility to our neighbor. We view it as a virtue necessary to keep us in our place.

While it is true that humility places us in right relationship with God and man, it is much more than that. It is godly behavior that goes hand in hand with love, kindness, compassion, and patience. Paul said that we act humbly when we, *"regard one another as more important than himself"* (Philippians 2:3). God acted with greater regard for us than for Himself when He gave His own Son to die for our sin. Can we accept that our creator is a humble God? God the Father loves us with a love that is greater than any father or mother could love. Jesus said, *"If you then, being evil, know how to give good gifts to your children, how much more will your Father who is in heaven give what is good to those who ask Him!"* (Matthew 7:11). Our humble God looks past the poor behavior of His children and gives. He looks past His requirement for righteousness and sends sun and rain on the just and the unjust.

Yes! God is our king. *"Be exalted, O God, above the heavens, and Your glory above all the earth"* (Psalm 108:5). He is also a God whose character includes **true humility**. In His power and authority, He offers this to us: *"Humble yourselves under the mighty hand of God, that He may exalt you at the proper time"* (1 Peter 5:6). Even while God the Father exalts us ,we continue to practice the virtue of humility.

Our Definition of Humility

Here is our definition from chapter one: Humility is an active approach to life involving the intentional choice of God and others above self, a determined avoidance of arrogance and pride, and the valuing of service and love far above power, prestige, or personal welfare. When we consider God's mercy and grace, we find our God to be one who chooses us over His righteous requirement to punish sin. When we examine God's role as our shepherd, we find God to be one who selflessly seeks us in our lost condition. When we think about God's love, we find God to be one who sacrificed His only Son to redeem us.

Again and again scripture describes God the Father with a humble character. 2 Corinthians 1:3-4 describes God as *"The Father of mercies and God of all comfort."* Psalm 68:5 describes God as *"a father of the fatherless and a judge for the widows."* In Psalm 63:7 the Psalmist says about God, *"For you have been my help, and in the shadow of Your wings I sing for joy."* Our God is more interested in loving us and caring for us than He is in condemning us or separating from us. Apostle Peter declares, *"Blessed be the God and Father of our Lord Jesus Christ, who according to His great mercy has caused us to be born again to a living hope through the resurrection of Jesus Christ from the dead"* (1 Peter 1:3).

Our God humbly waits for us to turn to Him. He doesn't force Himself on us, but reveals Himself to us and invites us to come to Him. Consider Isaiah 1:18. *"Come now, and let us reason together, says the Lord. Though your sins are as scarlet, they will be as white as snow. Though they are red like crimson, they will be like wool."*

The Love of God

God the Father loves God the Son. In the prayer of John 17, Jesus described for us and revealed to us the special relationship between himself and the heavenly Father. In verses 22 and 23 He said, *"The glory which You have given Me I have given to them, that they may be one, just as We are one; I in them and You in Me, that they may be perfected in unity, so that the world may know that You sent Me, and loved them, even as You have loved Me."* Jesus was and is God. The mystery of God in three persons makes it difficult to understand any sort of emotional expression of love from God the Father for God the Son, but we certainly see it.

When Jesus suffered and died on the cross, was it an emotionally painful moment for God the Father? As Son of God, Jesus was able to fulfill the requirement of sin by giving Himself as Holy sacrifice. It was no great feat for God, was it? God the Father would not have had the same emotions that the human mother Mary had, would He? Jesus, however, was fully God and fully man at the same time. He felt pain. He suffered fatigue. He knew the feeling of rejection, loneliness, and betrayal. He knew the pain and sorrow one feels when someone we love grieves for us. It was the humanness of Jesus that made possible His identification with man's suffering, but it was both the humanness and deity of Jesus that made possible emotional feelings. God is love. Emotions are good and given to man who is created in the image and likeness of God. God the Father loved the Son, who was God in the flesh with a love that is mysterious and impossible for our finite minds to understand. God the Father knew His son felt pain, fatigue and loneliness and humbly allowed His death.

God the Son was committed to carry out the good will of His Father, no matter the emotional pain it would cause them both. There was nothing simple or easy about the crucifixion event. The Holy and Righteous One bore our sins, touching sin as never before. As Jesus hung on the cross, emotions and feelings of horror and love, sorrow and love, agony and love, disgrace and love, brokenness and love, rejection and love, and pain and love were shared and swirling, engulfing, and fully involving the Three-In-One. The depth and breadth of the love between the Father and the Son and by the Godhead for the world, in the hours of the passion of Christ, could never be fully described or portrayed. Our inability to imagine the vastness of it leaves us unable to understand the degree of humility required to yield to the divine will that demanded a perfect sacrifice by the sinless one for a people who would never fully appreciate what was done. Jesus left His home in glory to reveal God's mercy, grace, and love through an act of humble submission to the requirement for blood to pay the penalty of our sin. It was a display of humility made possible by the greatest love the world has known. And, it all happened . . . for you and me.

Jesus' Example of The Humble Life

God the Son is our best picture of godly humility. He spoke about His nature and character in Matthew 11:29, *"Take my yoke upon you, and learn from me, for I am gentle and humble in heart, and you shall find rest for your souls."* There are many moments in Christ's life where we witness His gentleness and humility. We see it when He received the little children who had been pushed away by His disciples (Mark 10). It is not surprising that the disciples would consider the Lord's time far too important to be wasted upon children. They were protecting Him from the weariness that the clamor and commotion of a few hyperactive children can bring. But the Lord Jesus was not above spending time with little ones. His humble spirit enjoyed taking the tots upon his knee to caress them and bless them. Similarly, the humble Savior gave special attention to the wayward woman at the well and to a short and lonely Zaccheus. These and other examples demonstrate the boundless love, gentleness, and humility of God.

Humility is apparent when Jesus asked John to baptize Him in the Jordan (Matthew 3). John recognized the inverted position of that moment. He was not worthy to wipe the dust off the shoes of Jesus, let alone to plunge Him under muddy water. Jesus, who was without sin, humbly submitted to the arms of one who was numbered among sinners, to provide His example as a stamp of approval upon a symbolic act of repentance for sin. The picture of God's Son rising from the river, with Holy Spirit descending and the voice of God approving, moves us to delight in the meekness of God.

These are all gentle moments, but humility is found in powerful moments, as well. When He was in the middle of a needy crowd of people pushing and pulling, Jesus faced a woman who had been healed by merely touching the hem of his garment. With His kind reaction to her, we witness the miracle worker's humility. When Jesus took a little boy's lunch and served His disciples who then served a crowd of thousands bread and fish, it is a humble God-man who ensured that the people would not go hungry. Jesus very humbly approached society's outcast: the blind, lame, deathly sick, leprous, lonely, and the lost. *"Come to Me, all who are weary and heavy-laden . . ."* came from the lips of an humble Lord who reached out to those deemed by others to be ugly, repulsive, worthless, and a waste of time (Matthew 11:28).

We of course witness the humility of Jesus during His suffering and death as he faced His false accusers, a jeering crowd, the Sanhedrin, and Roman soldiers who slapped Him, spit on Him, beat Him and nailed Him to a cross. In His death He demonstrated humility for us. Jesus was not some weak, frail, fumbling, ignorant, unfortunate human being. He was God, and *"It was the Father's good pleasure for all the fullness of deity to dwell in Him"* (Colossians 1:19). Jesus had and has all power and glory. As He performed miracles and demonstrated his power and authority, He remained humble. He showed us the strength and power of humility. He showed us how humility serves God's purposes better than foolish pride. He showed us how to be godly and, like God, to be humble.

Humble As a Child

The picture of Jesus summoning children is one worth revisiting and staring at. On that day the face of Jesus already bore the burden of one who would soon describe to His followers His future suffering. He must have had a growing anticipation of the events that would culminate in His sacrifice for sin. The truths in the first chapter of the Gospel of John rested in the back of His mind. *"He was in the world, and the world was made through Him, and the world did not know Him. He came to His own, and those who were His own did not receive Him."* Yet, this God-man with a kind smile on his face allowed the children to touch and tug and roughhouse around Him.

What an amazing sight! Absorbed in the conversation that bounced from one child's story to another in a continuous stream of chatter without rhyme or reason, Jesus never looked away to see the lateness of the sun or to find if others were awaiting His care. He gave undivided attention to those precious lives. The grown-up world he set aside for a while. The children were important to him. He cared about their wants and wishes, and they knew it. They had waited for this moment to see him. He invited them up into his arms and scolded any adult who would impede them. *"Permit the children to come to Me, and do not hinder them, for the kingdom of God belongs to such as these"* (Luke 18:16).

There are many picture stories in the Bible where we witness the humility of Jesus. The scenes of His entry into Jerusalem on the back of a donkey, washing the disciples' feet, standing before the Sanhedrin, or hanging on that old rugged cross, all capture our veneration. These beautiful scenes of Jesus may go unnoticed for their demonstration of humbleness. But, placing ourselves in those moments we discover Jesus, The Son of God, taking steps each day toward Golgotha, with precious few years to prepare his disciples for their world-wide mission, verifying with every act and miracle the reality of His Messiah-ship, contending with hypocritical religious leadership and the forces of Satan, establishing His church, accomplishing the Father's will, and gently taking the small hands of a dirty little boy and giggly little girl to express his immeasurable love for them. We can hear Him speak to us. *"Whoever humbles himself as this child, he is the greatest in the kingdom of heaven"* (Matthew 18:4).

It may be that we ourselves must spend time with children before we can understand the essence of humility. Children bring us down to earth. Children challenge the high image we have of ourselves. Sitting on the floor and enjoying children and childish things require that we let go of ourselves and our need to be in control of life. Giving attention to children provides an orientation in humility. Perhaps when we finally leave the children to return to our adult world our clothes will still smell like humility and a humble aura will refuse to be hidden by our adult masks. In our awareness of the peculiar change in ourselves, maybe we will stop for a moment to humbly thank the Lord for those children.

The House of the Lord

Humility is an attitude which puts others ahead of our own concerns or welfare. God's humility is evident in the matter of the place of worship for the children of Israel. During the wilderness days, following the exodus from Egypt, God gave Moses instructions for the Tabernacle. This Tent of Meeting and its courtyard were constructed of goat's hair, ram's skins, porpoise skins, and linen. There were brass parts and gold and silver hooks and bands, with boards of acacia wood. Inside this Tent of Meeting was the Ark of the Covenant made of acacia wood and gold. Also in the tent was the table of showbread and the golden lampstand. In the courtyard were the bronze altar and laver.

The tent and its furnishings were made of fine and expensive materials. Of course! It was built as a dwelling place for God

Almighty. *"Let them construct a sanctuary for Me, that I may dwell among them"* (Exodus 25:8). The wilderness tabernacle was made as a portable dwelling. Each time God led His people to change locations, the tent and all things associated with it were packed up and carried. Amazingly, God's presence in the tabernacle was the signal to move.

> *"Then the cloud covered the tent of meeting, and the glory of the Lord filled the tabernacle. . . . Throughout all their journeys whenever the cloud was taken up from over the tabernacle, the sons of Israel would set out; but if the cloud was not taken up, then they did not set out until the day when it was taken up. For throughout all their journeys, the cloud of the Lord was on the tabernacle by day, and there was fire in it by night, in the sight of all the house of Israel." (Exodus 40:34, 36-38)*

So, you are wondering where humility is in all of this. David saw it. Around 450 years after the children of Israel no longer roamed the desert but inhabited the Promised Land, David noticed an incongruity.

> *"Now it came about when the king lived in his house, and the Lord had given him rest on every side from all his enemies, that the king said to Nathan the prophet, 'See now, I dwell in a house of cedar, but the ark of God dwells within tent curtains.'" (2 Samuel 7:1-2)*

David was ashamed that his house was finer than the house where God resided. After years of conquering the land and establishing His kingdom, he finally had free time to build a deserving house for God. God, however, did not give King David permission. That right would be reserved for David's son. Here is God's humble but authoritative response to David's desire:

"Wherever I have gone with all the sons of Israel, did I speak a word with one of the tribes of Israel, which I commanded to shepherd My people Israel, saying, 'Why have you not built Me a house of cedar?'" (2 Samuel 7:7)

God's words drip with humility like oil from David's beard. God miraculously protected and fed Israel in the desert. He led them to the land flowing with milk and honey. He revealed His love and mercy with every step. He provided judges to oversee the people's affairs and lead them. He gave the people a king at their request. He never left them nor forsook them. He gave them miraculous signs to assure them of His presence. He gave them ordinances to assure their forgiveness for sin. As the nation grew strong and prosperous, not once did He request a monument or temple. His request through the ages was for altars where He and those who worshiped Him could meet together for reconciliation. Every command was for their good. He is a good and loving God who asks us to put Him first in our lives, while He puts us first in His.

Mount Sinai

Even the order of business with Moses at Mount Sinai was an occasion where God put the needs of His people first. The Tabernacle was not the first order of business. First God sent Moses to tell the people His plan for them to be *"a kingdom of priests and a holy nation"* (Exodus 19:6). Then He gave the Ten Commandments and the Law. God's precepts were boundaries for living together in peace with God and fellow man. The Psalmist described them as he would describe a precious gift from God.

> *"The law of the Lord is perfect, restoring the soul; The testimony of the Lord is sure, making wise the simple. The precepts of the Lord are right, rejoicing the heart; The commandment of the Lord is pure, enlightening the eyes. ... The judgments of the Lord are true; they are righteous altogether. They are more desirable than gold, yes, than much fine gold; Sweeter also than honey and the drippings of the honeycomb. Moreover, by them Your servant is warned; In keeping them there is great reward." (Psalm 19:7-11)*

God dealt with matters involving everyday life before he presented His plan for priests. He explained how the people would settle offenses caused by cattle before He asked for offerings to construct His tent. He told how they should make restitution with a neighbor for a dead donkey before He gave the order for oils to anoint the ark. God was concerned that the people understand justice before they comprehend incense. God has always desired for His people to live in right relationship with each other. The prophet Micah reminds us of where God's priorities are.

> *"With what shall I come to the Lord and bow myself before the God on high? Shall I come to Him with burnt offerings, with yearling calves? Does the Lord take delight in thousands of rams, in ten thousand rivers of oil? Shall I*

present my firstborn for my rebellious acts,...? He has told you, O man, what is good; and what does the Lord require of you but to do justice, to love kindness, and to walk humbly with your God?" (Micah 6:6-8)

Our humble God, at the giving of the law, was thinking about us. That has never changed. He has always cared more about those in whom He breathed the breath of life than He cared about Himself. Jesus explained that one day the righteous will ask this question: *"Lord, when did we see You hungry, and feed You, or thirsty, and give You something to drink? And when did we see You a stranger, and invite You in, or naked, and clothe You? When did we see You sick, or in prison, and come to You?"* (Matthew 25:37-39). It is a humble God who will answer the question, *"... to the extent that you did it to one of these brothers of Mine, even the least of them, you did it to Me."*

A New Heaven and a New Earth

A final picture of the humility of God is found in *"The Revelation of Jesus Christ, which God gave Him to show to His bond-servants"* (Revelation 1:1). At the conclusion of this great vision Jesus gives to him, John writes the end of the story. After Satan is bound and after The Great White Throne Judgment, John witnessed a new heaven and earth, and a new Jerusalem. He heard a loud voice from the throne of God saying, *"Behold, the tabernacle of God is among men, and He will dwell among them, and they shall be His people, and God Himself will be among them, and He will wipe away every tear from their eyes . . ."* (Revelation 21:3-4).

Imagine this. A king notices one of his servants is sad. A closer look reveals a tear. The king is moved by the emotion he is witnessing. Rising from his throne, he quickly steps toward the servant. He lowers himself down to the floor where the commoner is sitting, flicks the tear away with his finger, and follows with a bear hug. He offers a gracious smile and then returns to his seat of authority. Would that be a humble scene? Would that require humility? I think so.

If that scene reveals humility, the scene at the end of the book in Revelation 21 is much more. God is in the house with his people. The Creator of the universe, the giver of life, our Lord and King, the all-powerful One, the all-knowing God will wipe away our tears. I can see Him moving from person to person, gently and humbly touching each tear, and hugging everyone. And then, He sees me. He sees the tears flowing down my cheeks. Suddenly He stands in front of me with a look that knows and understands my sorrow. He takes the sleeve of His royal robe and wipes my face, and then a warm embrace. My King! My Lord! That's humility.

CHAPTER TEN

EXERCISES IN HUMILITY

"Therefore, brethren, be all the more diligent to make certain about His calling and choosing you; for as long as you practice these things, you will never stumble; for in this way the entrance into the eternal kingdom of our Lord and Savior Jesus Christ will be abundantly supplied to you."
2 Peter 1:10-11

ಬಿ‍ಎಸ್

How do we know when we are humble? Take this biblical instruction for an example. *"If my people who are called by my name, humble themselves and pray . . ."* (2 Chronicles 7:14). Humble prayer is a prior condition to the promises that follow this admonition. When we enter into prayer, how do we know we are humble? We know we want to be. We know we should be. But, are we? Is there some quick gut check or some humble-ometer which would indicate the presence of humility as we begin our prayer? We could always check after the prayer. If God doesn't respond to our prayer, perhaps his lack of response means we lacked the required humility. However, we might have been very humble and His lack of positive response was due to something else. So, that isn't a reliable test.

Do we have an ability to recognize our own humbleness? Can our head and heart collaborate to generate a sincere attitude of true humility? To humble ourselves and pray is so much more than just praying. Praying can be nothing more than recitation.

To humble ourselves and pray is to become aware that our Father's eyes and ears are bent in our direction. Maybe we can be sure we are praying humbly when we have taken the time to bring our whole self before God: mind, body, and spirit. Our body is positioned to indicate humility. The words of our mouth are expressed with humility. Our spirit is humbled. Maybe also, as God is fully involved in hearing our prayer, His Spirit will indicate to our spirit that He is listening. Then we know. We are tuned into His voice, and through our prayer we hear Him.

Christian character develops and becomes more apparent as we exercise virtuous character traits. Love becomes more loving as we love often. We must begin rejoicing in the Lord before we can "rejoice in the Lord always" (Philippians 4:4). The more we trust the Lord, the more we are able to trust Him. The more we behave with humility, the more humility becomes the way we behave. Practice humility daily, and we will become the most humble person in the world. Whoaa! Obviously, if that is our goal, it will never happen. We practice humility because God calls us to a life of humility and because our humbleness pleases Him. We practice humility because we want to be more like Jesus.

The following exercises are intended to help us practice. Don't rush through this chapter. Take at least one day per exercise. There are fifteen, so it should take at least three weeks to complete them (you can skip weekends). Be careful. Exercising humility may develop "I" problems and sore knees. It can also assist us in drawing near to God. *"But to this one I will look, to him who is humble and contrite of spirit, and who trembles at My word"* (Isaiah 66:2).

Exercise #1: Praise

The greatest exercise in humility is praising God. King David was a man who knew that his strength and authority came from the Lord and that the strength of his relationship with the Lord was grounded in praise.

"My heart shall rejoice in Your salvation. I will sing to the Lord, because He has dealt bountifully with me."
(Psalm 13:6)

"Some boast in chariots and some in horses, but we will boast in the name of the Lord, our God." (Psalm 20:7)

"I will tell of Your name to my brethren; in the midst of the assembly I will praise You." (Psalm 22:22)

Praising God is a practice which stops the knee jerk reaction of praising ourselves. Pride wants to take credit for everything. Humble praise gives the credit for everything to God. The practice of praising God helps us avoid believing a lie and ties our minds and hearts to the truth. The lie is that we deserve glory and honor and praise. The truth is: *"For from Him and through Him and to him are all things. To Him be the glory forever, Amen"* (Romans 11:36).

Taking God for granted is arrogant and evil boasting. That is the way James described it.

> *"Come now, you who say, 'Today or tomorrow we will go to such and such a city, and spend a year there and engage in business and make a profit.' Yet you do not know what your life will be like tomorrow. You are just a vapor that appears for a little while and then vanishes away. Instead, you ought to say, 'If the Lord wills, we will live and also do this or that.' But as it is, you boast in your arrogance; all such boasting is evil." (James 4:13-16)*

In James 4:10 he said, *"Be humble in the presence of the Lord."* Our humility involves never assuming the goodness and provision of God, but acknowledging that all our hopes and plans are subject to the will of God.

Every day should be lived with the full awareness of God's sovereignty. The words of our supplication with God, our communication with others, and our contemplation with self, often indicate a degree in which we presume the activity of God in our lives. Every day we live without giving praise to God is a day when we take God for granted. Every morning we wake without praising God is a day begun without awareness of God's presence. With every blessing received, whether a cool breeze or renewed strength, if we fail to acknowledge God with praise, we presume upon His goodness. The habit of praise is an exercise in humility and necessary to prevent unintended boasting and self-glory. The above scripture from James teaches us to say, *"If the Lord wills."* We are also taught to say, "Praise the Lord," "To God be the glory," and "Amen," all of which are habits of those who are on life's journey with humility.

In a Psalm of repentance for sin, David cried to God, *"O Lord, open my lips, that my mouth may declare your praise. For You do not delight in sacrifice, . . . You are not pleased with burnt offering. The sacrifices of God are a broken spirit; a bro-*

ken and a contrite heart," (Psalm 51:15-17). Our sacrifices of praise are a practice in humility.

TODAY: Be aware of moments when you are prompted to praise. Keep a count of the number of praising-God moments in one eighteen-hour day. Record the number here. _____. Then, thank the Lord for opening your eyes to see His glory and your mouth to praise Him today.

Exercise #2: Be Thankful

Thankfulness and humility may be co-dependent. As we learn to be thankful for the things God has done, we learn something more about humility. Pride's focus is on self and overlooks what God has provided. *"For even though they knew God, they did not honor Him as God or give thanks"* (Romans 1:21). Humility is so aware of things outside of ourselves that we become more able to see the things which God has done and is doing.

A prayer is an exercise in humility. It may involve intentionally thinking about things for which we owe our gratitude. Or, we may simply be inspired by a sudden realization of something that evokes gratitude. When we take our eyes off man-made stuff and become aware of God-things, thankfulness happens and a prayer of thanks follows. Humility will be a natural bi-product.

Our prayers are too often hurried and repetitious. We thank God for things that come readily to mind and spend little effort reflecting and recalling the daily activity of God in our lives. For instance, this morning I observed the healing that was taking place with a sore on my hand. I paused to thank God for creating my body with an ability to heal. This afternoon I watched a bird fly overhead and thanked God for creating such amazing life to fill the earth.

As I further reflect, I am aware that there are many things for which I have never been thankful. I have thanked God for the sense of smell, but never for the particular aroma He gave to a rose, an orange, or my wife. I have thanked God for the sense of touch, but never for the particular feel of cotton, my cat, or my wife. I have thanked God for the ability to see, but never for the pleasure of seeing an ocean, an oak tree, or (you know what's coming next) my wife. I have thanked God for my church, but rarely for the people in my church who make me laugh, or challenge me to faithful service, or give me opportunity to be humble. I have thanked God for mission and purpose, but rarely have I thanked him for passion, unearned fruit, and more time.

The Psalmist meditated upon the works of the Lord. He says about God in Psalm 104:10-12, *"He sends forth springs in the valleys; they flow between the mountains; they give drink to every beast of the field; the wild donkeys quench their thirst, beside them the birds of the heavens dwell; they lift up their voices among the branches."* The Psalm ends with these words: *"I will sing praise to my God while I have my being. Let my meditation be pleasing to Him; As for me, I shall be glad in the Lord"* (Psalm 104:33-34).

Time taken for thankfulness and gratitude, directed toward an omnipotent, holy, and loving God, is time spent allowing our hearts to be humble. The great variety of sight and sound, touch and taste, that bombard us every moment is a luxury of life God created for each of us to enjoy. When any single ability to experience a small aspect of God's amazing display is gone, that loss brings with it the reality of how thankful we should have been before that color of God's rainbow disappeared. Be thankful for every color, every odor, every musical note, each different texture, each degree of temperature, each slight difference in flavor, every little whisper, each watt of light, every chill bump, every bit of wetness, each twinge of pain or ache, every little breeze or gust, every boom and ping, every mixture of harmony and every sour note, every shadow or brilliance of light, every stomach rumble, every warm wet kiss, every nose whistle or sneeze, each mouth full of sweet or sour, every itch, every scream, or bit of laughter, every field of clover or fresh spring shower, every wet dog, every moment with feet in mud or on sandy beach, each sight of butterfly or sparrow, each minute of worthwhile work, and every minute of restful sleep.

TODAY: Go outside in the morning. Spend five minutes giving thanks to God with your eyes open. Go outside in the afternoon. Spend five minutes giving thanks to God with your eyes open. Go outside after dark. Spend five minutes giving thanks to God with your eyes open. After each five-minute session, record the sweetest awareness you experienced.

Morning   _____
Afternoon _____
Evening   _____

Exercise #3: Thank Someone

Why do we sometimes have such difficulty saying *thank you*? It is painful at times to say these words. Why? Are we afraid that saying *thanks* acknowledges a debt? Do we think we may now owe a good deed in return for the good deed done? Because we don't want to owe anyone anything, we refuse to acknowledge that anything out of the ordinary, worthy of a *thank you,* was accomplished. We stubbornly refuse to see what others do that might deserve a thank you. Maybe part of the problem is that we might realize how little good we do compared to what others around us are doing. Or, maybe saying *thank you* acknowledges good in some one which we don't want to admit. We would rather think of that person in negative terms. Saying *thanks* would spoil the image we want to maintain of them. These are each crazy reasons to fail to offer someone thanks.

All contrived reasons for not saying *thanks* are attached to sinful pride. Any moment in which we have difficulty saying *thank you* becomes for us a signal that we are not in our humble mode. Saying *thank you* is a wonderful exercise in humility. Say it. Say it and mean it. *Thank you!* You are so kind to have done this thing. Thank you very much. Now, doesn't that feel better? We became humble in the moment instead of prideful. It will be easier next time. We may even begin to discover that being thankful for every little thing others do is not accumulating debt, but encouraging right action in others. There may be ministry done in saying *thank you*. We may get great reward and deserve great recognition for the humility we display by saying *thank you*. Perhaps God will pour out rich blessings on us because we are such grateful people. Oops! Now we are headed in a non-humble heading aren't we? It is so difficult to remain humble.

TODAY: Think of two people who are very difficult for you to thank. Thanking them would require true humility. The more difficult, the more humility is involved. Who are they? _____ and _____
Now go and do it!

Exercise #4: "kneeling down on the beach" Acts 21:5

What is it about kneeling when we pray that is an act and an exercise in humility? There are many references in the Bible about kneeling in prayer. The one we mentioned in an earlier chapter was regarding the prayer practices of Daniel. "*...and he continued kneeling on his knees three times a day, praying and giving thanks before his God, as he had been doing previously,*" (Daniel 6:10).

Kneeling is very clearly an appropriate position for prayer, but we resist doing it. We don't want to be seen doing it. That resistance is called pride. The best remedy for sinful pride is practicing humility.

Kneeling before a king is done to show submission to the king's authority and to honor him as king. Bowing down before the king is a show of one's allegiance to the king and readiness to serve him. Kneeling in prayer to God is all that. Jesus is our king. One day soon, "*at the name of Jesus every knee will bow, ... and every tongue will confess that Jesus Christ is Lord, to the glory of God the Father*" (Philippians 2:9-11). We do not wait for "one day." We bow before Him now.

TODAY: All that is asked for in this exercise is that you find a moment today for a prayer on your knees. You are not expected to do this *"on the beach"* as in the quote from Acts 21:5. I challenge, however, sometime when you are on a public beach where others may see you, being careful not to pray *"to be noticed by them"* (Matthew 6:1), but doing it only as an experience in true humility before God, kneel in prayer. After you pray on your knees today, ask yourself, "How did that feel?"

Exercise #5 Love Your Enemy

There is humility in right behavior. An example of this is found in scriptural instructions regarding our enemies. It is easy to see the humility involved in the guidance given by the writer of Proverbs. *"Do not rejoice when your enemy falls, and do not let your heart be glad when he stumbles; Or the Lord will see it and be displeased"* (Proverbs 24:17-18). Arrogance and haughtiness belong to the one who takes pleasure in the pain of his opponent. An attitude of joy over the troubles of any person is wrong. When humility hears about the calamity or heartache of an enemy, it reacts with compassion and empathy. Proverbs 25:21 advises, *"If your enemy is hungry, give him food to eat; and if he is thirsty, give him water to drink."* Why? Because this is right and godly behavior.

If scripture admonishes us to be humble (and it does), then we must treat our enemies with kindness. Jesus calls us to this humble behavior when He commands, *"You have heard that it was said, 'You shall love your neighbor and hate your enemy.' But I say to you 'You shall love your enemies and pray for those who persecute you, so that you may be sons of your Father who is in heaven;'"* (Matthew 5:43-45). One of the most challenging displays of humility given us by our Lord also comes from Matthew 5 which is, *"whoever slaps you on your right cheek, turn the other to him also"* (Matthew 5:39). Who among us has that much humility, we might ask? Our answer is: only those who love the character of our Lord Jesus and are firmly committed to His command to be humble servants. The wise author of Proverbs reminds us once more of this. *"When a man's ways are pleasing to the Lord, He makes even his enemies to be at peace with him"* (Proverbs 16:7). Our wrong behavior toward an enemy, which includes rejoicing when he stumbles and crumbles, could be a bit humiliating when God changes the heart of that enemy and brings him to us as a brother.

TODAY: Who has an adversarial relationship with you? _____ Pray for him or her for seven minutes. Name the person out loud. Pray only for one enemy and for no less than seven minutes. You may pray longer than seven minutes if compelled. While you proceed each day with a new exercise, continue this one for six more days. There is no magic in the number seven. Your enemy needs prayer, and you need the practice.

Exercise #6: A Random Act of Humility

A book I enjoy leafing through now and then is titled, *List Your Self, List-making as the Way to Self-Discovery*. It is three hundred pages of lines with the list title at the top of each page. The book touts itself as "A provocative, probing and personal expedition into your mind, heart, and soul."[32] That, of course, is only true if the reader probes provocatively and personally into their mind, heart and soul to create the various lists suggested. For me it is a very enjoyable exercise in personal reflection. I had fun with, "List all the things you've made or built by hand." Also, "List all the things you'd like to say to your mother" was good therapy. I have added to that list many times. I have been contemplating a new list for myself called, "List all the places you've been that made you feel immortal, invincible, or omnipotent."

The last grouping of lists in this book is called, *Suddenly*. I haven't made any of these yet. One is called, *Suddenly you can*

---

[32] Ilene Segalove and Paul Bob Velick, *List Your Self:Listmaking as the Way to Self-Discovery* (Kansas City: Andrews and McMeel, 1996), cover.

talk to animals. List the ones you want to converse with and why. I have a very large plecostomus. I would love to know what is on his or her mind. How about that slug on the porch? If I could talk to it, what could it tell me about humility and how long would it take the slug to tell me?

If it is in the book, I haven't found it, but it would be interesting to make a daily list of my personal acts of humility. Can we claim humility if we can't point to an act of humility? This may be a similar situation to what the book of James says about faith and works. *"Show me your faith without the works, and I will show you my faith by my works"* (James 2:18). Do humility and works function the same way? If we can't identify an act of humility in our day's activity, can we consider ourselves humble? Is humility without humble acts worthless humility? A list could help. A conscious effort to perform an act of humility in order to have something to add to a humility list could encourage more humble behavior. Let's at least test it.

TODAY: Contrive and commit an intentionally humble act today. Then, write out what you did, and explain why you think it was a demonstration of humility. Writing it out is part of the exercise.

Exercise #7: Embarrass Yourself

How humble can we be? How low can we go? What is the most menial service we can render? What are the limits of our humility? No, I am not suggesting a contest, only a self-examination. Is there an act of humility which we would refuse to do because our self-esteem or residual pride would not allow it? Some introspection may provide interesting self-discovery.

Which of these actions would we avoid and have an iron-clad excuse for not doing? — enter an extremely dirty and bug-infested home to visit a poor family, change someone else's baby's diaper, change the diaper of an adult who cannot do it for himself, spoon-feed a handicapped person, say nothing when an untruth is told about you in front of your peers, perform CPR on a homeless person to include mouth to mouth, adopt a teenager, tip the cable-guy, ask for prayer, hug a cranky old man or woman, carry your wife's purse, volunteer to ring the bell at the Salvation Army Christmas kettle, allow yourself to cry, wear something that your peers would consider un-cool, raise your hands in church as an act of praise, help a morbidly heavy person get out of a car, mentor a troubled elementary student, compliment the pastor, volunteer to read to a coma patient, shave your head out of empathy for a cancer patient, or talk to a stranger about Jesus.

I interrupt the list to give us a chance to breathe. If none of the above were beyond the limits of our humility, what about one of these? — make friends with the most unpopular person you know, sing karaoke for a nursing home, drive the speed-limit, point out a character flaw to a friend, suffer silently, pick up someone else's trash, or kiss a mule?

Is it possible that the excuses we offer for shunning some of these things actually hide a boat-load of pride? Some of these we may avoid because they are stupid. Which of these things would Jesus refuse? Jesus said *"Whoever exalts himself shall be humbled; and whoever humbles himself shall be exalted"* (Matthew 23:12). He then launches into several verses describing the pride of the hypocrite; pride which represses the kind of care and concern for others which He expects from His disciples. What act of submission to the will of God for us has gone undone because we lack the humility required? Here is an even better question. What blessing has our pride insidiously stolen from us?

TODAY: Do something that would normally embarrass you. Do not apologize for being embarrassed. Make it a selfless act. Do not draw attention to yourself. Just be humble and do it. What will it be? _____.

When finished, record what was done, the date and time, and how much pride was lost.

_____
_____
_____

Exercise #8: Humble Hearing

Humble hearing makes conversation immensely more pleasurable. A little humility attributes value to thoughts expressed by the other half of the dialogue. A complete lack of humility only values the other person's role to listen and cares nothing about hearing what is on their mind. It doesn't usually take long to recognize when a conversation is one sided. We are expected to listen and make no more response than to say, "Really!" or "Uh huh, yes, wow!" The dialogue is actually a monologue and we have been rendered unimportant except to be used as a receptacle for dumping their trash. Frustration comes when we are left out of what we thought was an invitation to share.

We can do nothing to fix these pompous, egoistical, self-absorbed windbags. We can do something about ourselves. We can make sure that we are humble when chatting with others. Humility speaks with thoughtfulness and consideration and listens with respect and attention. Humility desires true dialogue and enjoys the give and take. It enjoys the connection made when conversing. Conversation is more than an opportunity to showcase one's ability to entertain. It is opportunity to relate and bond.

Good conversation with healthy discussion and enjoyable dialogue requires courteous give and take with each person practicing the art of good listening and respectful interjection. I agree with a pastor friend of mine who commented to his congregation that he loved good *intercourse*. His audience laughed, probably because they weren't accustomed to hearing the word used except when attached to the word *sexual*. *Intercourse* has to do with connecting. *Verbal intercourse*, of course, is dual discourse with an exchange of thoughts and ideas. Conversation can be almost as pleasurable as the other sort of intercourse when proper rules of encounter are observed.

Humility and pride are easily recognized by the careful observer of any conversation. The prideful participant bullies his way through the conversation taking advantage of every topic to display his knowledge. She cares nothing about the input of others and finds it difficult to patiently wait her turn. He is unaware when he begins to speak that another person was in the middle of a story or idea. Pride drives her to dominate and control what had begun as conversation but crumbled into a singular performance. If he performs well, people will give him their attention for a short time. Dialogue doesn't happen when the prideful person is in the room; only monologue.

A little humility makes for great intercourse. Humility sets self aside to enjoy the minds of other people. For the humble person, questions are offered as often as attempted answers. The humble want to know what others think as much as they want others to know what they are thinking. They keep the conversation going, involving every person present, sharing, learning, listening, observing, minds whirling, hands and arms waving, spirits connecting, hearts beating, emotions stirring, passions teased, personalities entangled, and time flies until finally the chatter begins to subside, and everyone involved is tired and satisfied. That experience cannot happen if pride walks into the middle of it. Humility provides for sweet encounters and delightful conversation, which is one more reason why I prefer humble living.

TODAY: During some conversation time today, become aware of the dynamics of the interaction. Be most conscious of how you are involved and involving others. Enjoy the other persons in the conversation without a desire to dominate. Make the other persons in the conversation the center of your attention. After the conversation, on a scale of 1 to 10, record how pleasurable that conversation was. _____

Exercise #9: Saying "I'm Sorry"

Is an admission of fault a sign of strength or weakness? Even when uttered in anger with great reluctance, the words *I was wrong* can fall from the lips only when dislodged by humility. Pride will resist admission of a wrong even if it is completely useless and senseless to do so. What is there to gain by refusing to accept blame or admit guilt? Is denial expected to preserve one's image or reputation? Do we sometimes suppose that people will reject us if they discover we make mistakes? Will our self-confidence or courage collapse if we confess a wrong done or other failure? When we witness a poor sap defaming his self or degrading herself by insisting on innocence in the face of obvious error, we witness the insanity and desperation of pride.

No one is impressed or bedazzled by the person who cannot say *I'm sorry*. He instead reveals incredible weakness and discredits himself far more than any public apology will. A willingness to unashamedly humble ourselves and acknowledge our indiscretions is far more admirable and notable. Any loss of pride during public acknowledgement of misconduct is instantly regained by the estimable character that compels us to humbly confess. Humility protects us from the humiliation suffered when pride is incapable of saying such words as, "Oops, I did it again." Stand tall with pride and stumble. Or, be strong, bow low, be humble.

It isn't easy to say *I'm sorry*. It is even harder when we buy into the philosophy a lot of people have that saying *I'm sorry* isn't something we should do. Some people believe that if what we have done has bothered someone else, we shouldn't lose sleep over it. It's their problem. They (those who have been offended) ought to get over it. Various schools of thought encourage us to build our own self-esteem by rejecting any feelings of personal guilt, blame or shame. Saying *I'm sorry,* they say, is the admission of a mistake which reinforces negative feelings about ourselves. They believe high self-esteem is to be achieved by a positive focus that cannot see any negative.

Once we have fully adopted the practice of removing the words *I'm sorry* from our vocabulary, we have succeeded in conflicting our spiritual life. Now what do we do? We can no longer see ourselves as sinners nor consider any of our actions to require confession and forgiveness. Unless! Unless we could somehow carefully separate our lives into two worlds: our everyday lives and our religious lives. That could work! We could be totally guiltless with gigantic feelings of self-worth in our *normal* everyday life. We could save a little piece of our psyche in which to allow our spiritual life the luxury of humility that acknowledges sin and allows our lips to form the words I'm sorry to a forgiving God.

Dividing ourselves into two persons could solve an enormous amount of conflict in our lives. It could be like having the best of both worlds. We could be both spiritual and worldly at the same time. We could be humble and proud, Cane and Abel, saints and ain'ts . . . godly and godless. Or ... maybe not. Maybe we can learn that adopting the philosophy of rejecting guilt is pagan, non-Christian philosophy. We need to reunite body, soul, and spirit under the authority of almighty God. Perhaps that only happens by learning the strength that comes when we are willing to confess when we are wrong. *"Confess your sins to one another, and pray for one another so that you may be healed."* (James 5:16).

TODAY: Learn the freedom and relief of saying I'm sorry. There is probably an apology you have been avoiding. Humble-up, drop the cover-up, face the one you offended, and say it! Then admit that there is someone else to whom you should have apologized first. Don't let the sun go down before you have told them, *I'm sorry*.

To whom did you apologize? _____

Exercise #10: Sacrificing Freedoms

Voluntarily giving up personal freedoms requires two giant scoops of humility. I am not referring to the kind of freedom for which we should fight, such as freedom from tyranny, slavery, abuse, fear, oppression, and taxes (just kidding about the taxes). Our Declaration of Independence declares that "all Men are . . . endowed by their Creator with certain unalienable rights, that among these are Life, Liberty, and the Pursuit of Happiness."

We should never give away those freedoms. We do have the freedom, however, to individually sacrifice some personal freedoms in order to ensure that freedom itself is maintained for our children and our children's children. Securing rights and freedom requires the voluntary sacrifice of some personal freedoms.

The D of I concludes, "And for the support of this Declaration, with a firm Reliance on the Protection of divine Providence, we mutually pledge to each other our Lives, our fortunes, and our sacred Honor." Our founding fathers knew that protecting the freedoms of a nation requires that humble men and women of that nation devote time, personal resources, career path, energy, blood, sweat, and tears to preserve freedom.

Many of our countrymen and women understand personal sacrifice. The soldier or Marine is not free to lie on a beach in Florida while he or she accepts combat duty. The sailor is not free to go home after work to a devoted husband or wife while assigned duty aboard a ship in foreign seas. The airman is not free to catch the newest movie with friends at the hometown theatre while serving as a part of a security force. The Coastie does not have the freedom to lovingly kiss a son or daughter goodnight on those evenings when he or she is faithfully patrolling American waters. Police officers do not have the freedom to kick back on the couch for a relaxing night of TV when their shift requires them to maintain the peace on Main Street, USA. There are many other men and women who make daily sacrifices of personal freedoms to guard our rights and liberty. They are firefighters, forest rangers, border patrol, FBI agents, and prison guards. They are also State representatives, Senators, and even the United States President who will sacrifice sleep to answer the phone at 3 o'clock in the morning.

There is a mixture of pride and humility that keeps all these people at their post. There is pride in the accomplishments of many Americans who have gone before them to secure our freedom. There is humility in undertaking a task that carries so much responsibility. There is pride in personal heroes who inspired their choices. There is humility in attempting to be someone else's hero. There is pride in belonging to a nation of people who genuinely care about each other and the people of the world. There is humility in trying to live up to the trust those people have placed in us. There is pride for living in a land of freedom, opportunity, and prosperity. There is humility in the realization that the continuation of that freedom, opportunity and prosperity may depend on how well we respond to every threat. For a free nation's future to be tightly encased and brightly faced and never erased, pride must be rightly placed and humility Godly based and personal freedoms lightly embraced. The third stanza of the song "America," written by Katharine Lee Bates, illustrates these ideals with these familiar words:

> O beautiful for heroes prov'd
> In liberating strife
> Who more than self their country lov'd
> And mercy more than life!
> America! America!
> May God thy gold refine
> Till all success be nobleness
> And ev'ry gain divine!

TODAY: Answer these two questions: (1) What sacrifices have I made to preserve the freedoms and God-given rights of others? (2) Am I humble enough to care more about others than myself? Find an active member of the U.S. Armed Services, or a police officer, or a fireman, or a nurse, or a local judge to tell them thank you for keeping our nation strong. Avoid letting political or philosophical ideals dilute your sincere appreciation.

What is the name of the person to whom you spoke? _____ How did you express your appreciation?

_____

Exercise #11: Regard The Lowly Regarded

Humility is both an attitude and an act. Attitude cannot help but produce action which is consistent with the attitude. The reverse is sometimes true. A conscious decision to perform a humble act may encourage and bring about an attitude of humility. Exercises in humility assist us in developing and strengthening that attitude as our default attitude. Try this exercise based on Philippians 2:3 *"Do nothing from selfishness or empty conceit, but with humility of mind let each of you regard one another as more important than himself."*

This exercise involves picking a person whom we will intentionally treat as more important than ourselves. Obviously, not much humility would be required to regard someone as more important who really is more important than we are. That would be too simple. If we are somewhat normal and are able to distinguish between persons greater than us and those lesser than us, then this exercise may be do-able.

The biblical instruction is to put others first, letting them have first consideration. Can we do that? Are we able to consider the needs of a subordinate or someone junior to us ahead of our own needs? What about someone who might be regarded as far less important than we are? The command to regard others as more important than ourselves should encompass a large span of people, to include those in a much lower social status, those who contribute much less to society, those who are less healthy and fit, those who are less intelligent, and those who have made poorer life decisions. These are the people we are expected to regard as more important. Humility of mind involves treating with high regard even those who are the least valued by others. Our high regard for them should not result in behavior that delights in our high regard.

TODAY: Pick a person with whom you have regular contact, who has considerably less income, ability, charm, intelligence or social status. This should be a person you would not normally choose to be on your team. Determine to act toward that person in a way that would sincerely indicate high regard. You must do something with them or for them that involves putting their interests ahead of your own.

Who is that person? _____
What did you do?
_____
Date completed: _____

Exercise #12: The Gentlemen and Lady

Neither a gentleman or lady, nor the desire to be one is much in vogue today. It is rare to find a real gentleman or lady. Few men and women aspire to exhibit good manners and observe proper etiquette. Theodore Roosevelt allegedly said, "Courtesy is as much a mark of a gentleman as courage." It seems it was not so long ago that we in America valued being a gentleman or lady and knew the value of "courtesy." Good manners seem to have gone out of style.

In the days of the life of Martin Luther King, Jr. a pledge was drafted for those protesting in demonstrations in Birmingham.

They signed a commitment to ten commandments of the nonviolent movement. The 6th commandment was to, "observe with both friend and foe the ordinary rules of courtesy."[33] Civility, humility, and courtesy are necessary in every endeavor.

Ordinary rules of courtesy and the art of being a lady or a gentleman always require humility. One list of what it takes to be a gentleman included these: 1. Be polite. 2. Do not curse. 3. Do not speak loudly. 4. Do not lose your temper. 5. Do not stare. 6. Do not interrupt. 7. Do not spit. 8. Do not laugh at others' mistakes. And, 9. Remove your hat indoors. If these are old fashioned, it is because manners have unfortunately become outdated, as has the nobleness of gentlemanliness.[34]

Sometime before he turned sixteen, George Washington compiled a list of 110 Rules of Civility and Decent Behavior.[35] These timeless principles reveal that an element of humility was once commonly part of proper behavior. Here are just a few of his rules:

> Rule 1. Every act done in company ought to be with some sign of respect to those that are present.
> Rule 65. Speak not injurious words neither in jest nor earnest; scoff at none although they give occasion.
> Rule 68. Give not advice without being asked and when desired, do it briefly.
> Rule 70. Reprehend not the imperfections of others, for that belongs to parents, masters, and superiors.
> Rule 74. When another speaks, be attentive yourself and dis-

---

[33] Martin Luther King, Jr., *The Words of Martin Luther King, Jr.*, comp. Coretta Scott King (New York: Newmarket Press, 1987), 74.

[34] http://www.askmen.com/money/successful/41_success.html

[35] George Washington, *George Washington's Rules of Civility and Decent Behavior in Company and Conversation*, (Bedford, MA: Applewood Books, 1988), p.9-30.

turb not the audience. If any hesitate in his words, help him not nor prompt him without desired. Interrupt him not, nor answer him till his speech be ended.

A study of all of Washington's rules reveals that each has to do with putting people before our own self-gratification. That attitude is what we are seeking and seem to rarely find. That is what we are calling **true humility**.

TODAY: Buy a book of etiquette or a book of manners. Adopt just one manner or rule of etiquette not previously practiced, and make it yours. What new manner did you select?

Exercise #13: Commitment To Assemble

Material things keep us from being humble. They don't have to. We can have lots of material things and still be humble, but we like things too much. We love things. Things become a source of pride. When our things are bigger and better than their things, we gloat over them. When we have the best of something, we begin to think more highly of ourselves. Look at us! We have the best one of these ever made. *Things* become our joy. Without this *thing* or that *thing,* we are unhappy. When we have these *things,* we are extremely happy. Our joy begins to depend upon how many *things* we have that are bigger, better, and best. Self-centeredness views *things* as trophies. *Things* become the center of our lives. Humility is a critical attitude for the believer because it guards us against a selfishness that wants to worship *things*. We must fight the desire to make *things* our god, remember who made *things,* and from whence cometh *things*. The Lord's Day Sabbath becomes key in this inner battle. Giving a day out of seven to the Lord is an exercise in humility and a weekly realigning of our priorities. Sunday is a day to tear down our golden *thing* to stand humbly before the only true God. The Prophet Isaiah writes,

> *"If because of the Sabbath, you turn your foot from doing your own pleasure on My holy day, and call the Sabbath a delight, the holy day of the Lord honorable, and shall honor it, desisting from your own ways, from seeking your own pleasure, and speaking your own word, then you will take delight in the Lord." (Isaiah 58:13-14)*

The Lord should be our greatest joy. When we get attached to *things,* they displace God in our lives and become our joy. Sunday is a day when it becomes clear who or what is our god. We can disagree and defend our actions all day long, but our actions reveal what things rule us. We must fight back against our own selfish spirit and attitude by not allowing things to crowd God out of our lives.

TODAY: Commit yourself to remove stuff from your calendar that prevent you from assembling together with believers to worship the Lord every Sunday. Do not miss church this week. The commitment to assemble for worship is an exercise in humility.

Exercise #14: Everyday People

We cross paths with humble people every day. Do you believe that? We like to imagine our world as devoid of any truly humble people. Are there actually none, or are we just incapable of seeing them when they are staring us in the face? Please note, I am not speaking about perfect people. We are looking today for humility embodied in everyday people.

The question is, can you recognize humility when you see it? At this point in our study and our immersion in ideas, thoughts and examples of humility, we should be able to spot humility in strangers on the street. When we think we have observed humility in someone's behavior, it may require an encounter with that person to affirm our suspicion. Be careful. I must give you a scriptural warning. *"Do not neglect to show hospitality to strangers, for by this some have entertained angels without knowing it"* (Hebrews 13:2). I suspect angels are humble.

TODAY: Remember! A day of watching for signs of humility in everyday people whom we may or may not know is a day of thinking about and learning more about humility. It is a good day! Pray for God to assist you in your search. When you see one (sounds like we are searching for a four-leafed clover … but we are not), after as much observation and investigation as you feel comfortable, answer this question: Does this person excite you or repulse you?

Exercise #15: My Life in Review

Chapter eleven of this book is titled, "Humility in the phases of my life." This chapter is my reflection on my life as I recall the part humility has played throughout the various phases of life. It is my discovery of the power of humility to provide strength and joy. After you finish reading chapter eleven, I encourage you to do the same.

SOMEDAY: Write down moments throughout your life when you acted with humility, when a humble person impacted your life, when you wish you had been more humble, or when the hand of God humbled you. Compile a simple list of life lessons regarding humility. Share your list with me or someone near and dear. Do not try to find the angel you met on the street. He or she (probably a she) will not admit to being an angel.

Everyday Opportunities To Practice Humility

God gives us opportunity to act humbly every day. He gives us moments to step down from our high estimation of ourselves. One day at church, in the middle of a crowd of people, my friend who has cerebral palsy asked me to tie her shoes. I gladly tied them, and later thought about what a humble act that was. That sounds like I'm bragging about my humility. I only mention it as an example of one of those small opportunities to act humbly. We need those to keep us humble.

We should look for them throughout our day: the opportunity to hold a child's hand, to clean up someone else's mess, to listen to someone whom we might deem unimportant, to congratulate someone on a minor achievement, to pay a compliment to someone we normally avoid, to swallow the criticism on the tip of our tongue, to hear someone speak incorrectly and not correct them, to say the words *I'm sorry* or *excuse me* or *thank you*, to accept someone else's help, to bow in prayer by yourself in a restaurant without regard to how others may view us, to give the garbage collector a Coke, to say *I love you* to the pastor and mean it, to allow a slower car to break in front of you in traffic without retribution, to call someone who you have been refusing ever to talk to again, and even to tie someone's shoe who is unable to do it for herself.

When thoughts about humility are more frequent than thoughts about ourselves, and acts of humility are as common as those daily tasks of personal care, we will still need to continue the exercise of selfless living to keep pernicious pride at bay. Be humble!

HUMILITY IN THE PHASES OF MY LIFE

"Good and upright is the Lord; therefore He instructs sinners in the way. He leads the humble in justice, and He teaches the humble His way."
Psalm 25:8-9

~~~

Life! Not only is it not a bed of roses, it sometimes won't even produce pansies. This doesn't mean that life is inevitably impossible, or that pansies are less valuable than roses, but that life is always a challenge, especially for the living. The road of life consists of many troublesome twists and turns. The care with which we navigate each corner and juncture determines how smoothly we complete each section of our course. Whether we are in a humble or prideful mode as we maneuver through each new phase of life will make a difference. I recommend a time of reflection in which you look at your life story to observe how pride or humility has impacted your journey. Allow me to use my own life to illustrate. I am most knowledgeable about the bends and bumps I have encountered and the power of humility for me.

Humility is the skill of moving self out of the way. That never gets easy because each phase is of itself so different and differently difficult. I love the illustration of the woman who was smiling as she observed another mother's child pitching a fit. Her husband asked if she knew the young girl she was watching. She replied, "I don't believe I know her, but her phase sure looks familiar." Perhaps some of the phases I now describe will look familiar to you.

A Call To Ministry

I accepted the call of God to the gospel ministry as I turned nineteen. I first consulted my pastor about what I believed were milestones and markers. I explained how my parents and grandparents had intimated their expectations of God's plan for me throughout my childhood years. Their comments influenced my thinking, but I always suspected their words to be merely their wishes and not necessarily God's. My relationship with God was close from the age of ten. That is when I understood that I could not rely upon godly parents or church-going to receive salvation and an eternal home with God. With sincere prayer, I confessed my sin and committed my life to follow Jesus. My new life in Christ began with that humble decision. Afterward, I became more and more aware of God's work in me.

As I spoke with my pastor about what I believed God wanted me to do, I shared various experiences which seemed to confirm what God was saying to me during my Bible reading and daily prayer. The thought of entering some preaching and pastoral ministry had become inescapable for me. This was not without some conflicting signs. One was my extremely shy personality that had always interfered with any positive experience of standing before even the smallest crowd. The other was that I had already enlisted in the Navy (to avoid being drafted into the ranks of foot soldiers bound for Vietnam) and would leave for Boot Camp in July. If God was now calling me into the preaching ministry, why did He create me with such a timid spirit, and why did He allow me to join the military?

My pastor did not confirm my calling, but neither did he deny it. He wisely avoided making the decision for me. He listened, probed, and then gave this advice: "Norman, if you can do anything other than the preaching and pastoral ministry, do it!" One week later, I made a public decision. I walked up to the pastor who stood in the front of the church during a hymn of invitation and said, "I don't know why, and I don't know how, but I can't do anything else. God is calling me to ministry." I appreciated then the practice of my church to invite public professions. The sense of finality which comes when making a decision in front of others, helps to discourage any decision unless one is certain, and carries the possibility of future embarrassment for one who might later have a change of mind.

God is amazing. He took away some of my timidity, but left enough to keep me humble. He used my initial years in the Navy to show me where He wanted me to do ministry. Humility assists us with those decisions that require great confidence in God. We humbly accept His direction into the unknown. Pride wants God to provide more evidence before making a move. Humility hops aboard God's ship and says, "I'm ready to get underway, Sir. Just give the command, and we'll cast off." There were three years of Naval service, four years of college and three years of seminary before I finally entered full-time ministry. Humility made the waiting easier to endure, while pride fought me the entire ten-year journey.

My Life Partner

Marriage isn't always met with humility. It happens most often when we are young and full of ourselves. When a pretty young girl agreed to be my partner for life, how could I avoid letting pride be in charge? God gave me enough wisdom to know that marriage is more than just being married. It is a partnership. That partnership can be an enjoyable one or a resentful one. Pride drives a person to put himself first. When a partner cares most about his own way, his needs, his toys, his time, his friends, his career, and his money, he will resent and be angry at the partner who demands consideration and inclusion. When humility is missing in the character of one partner, the only way the marriage can survive is if the other partner is totally humble, totally selfless. Without a little humility in both bride and groom, the marriage may succeed in avoiding divorce, but will never be much more than survival.

A true partnership exists when both partners share the corporation. The marriage union was created by God to be two lives fused into one. A couple will never know the beauty, pleasure, and fulfillment of marriage until they unselfishly receive and commit to each other. The relationship must be allowed to become bigger and more important than each individual in it. Each must move self out of the way and cling to the other.

The day I watched my beautiful wife walk down the aisle on the arm of her father to stand beside me before our pastor, was the day I pledged to be humble. "I take you, Connie, to be my wife, to have and to hold, to love, honor, and cherish, from this day forward, for better or worse, till we are parted by death." The marriage vow is a promise to look at life differently. My life, from that day forward, was not about me. It was about us. If she and I can sincerely accept and believe that, we will have humbly entered a new phase of life that will provide tremendous joy.

A Naval Career?

After ten years of preparation, I fully expected to serve at least 20 years in the Navy chaplaincy. A minister must fulfill the requirements of his endorsing agency in order to make application for a commission into the military branch of his choice.

Most of the mainline Christian denominations have an office that reviews and endorses ministers to represent them. All of the agencies have similar expectations: a bachelor's degree, a seminary degree and two years of full-time pastoral ministry after the completion of seminary. Of course, there are papers to write and forms to submit.

Connie and I married after both of us finished our bachelor's - hers in nursing and mine in religion. We took a year after college to earn just enough to pay off some debt before moving to Texas to enter seminary. If it were not for the chaplaincy requirement, I probably would never have attempted a master's degree. We were committed to our Navy goal, so we endured three and half years of studies, separation from family, and living near the poverty level. Connie gave birth to our first child in a little West Texas town far from home. I drove 90 miles each way to school for the privilege of serving as Youth Minister in our county-seat town. They were good years, and we humbly thank the Lord for them and for God's people who loved us along the way. With that step completed, we looked for a church to pastor.

God provided a pastoral call to a beautiful little country church in Alabama. For the second time, we discovered after a self-move that Connie was expecting. We were living only two hours away from our parents for the birth of our second child. It was great to have family near. I was Pastor for two years, and I could not have asked for a more enjoyable first pastorate. It would have been easy to remain there longer, but I was nearing the Navy's age cutoff. It was time to go.

Many Christians have discovered that following God's direction can mean sacrifice and hardship. That is why humility is so vital. When faced with decisions that will involve years of struggles that will seem unfair to wife and children, and all of this just to finally reach the beginning of a life that will require more sacrifice and hardship, one must keep remembering: It's not about me, and it isn't about us. We must move ourselves out of the way and put God first. That's humility.

I learned during chaplain's school, my initial entry training, that newly passed federal legislation removed any guarantee of remaining in the military to the completion of twenty years. The Navy and other branches of service had moved to an up-or-out system. Failure to receive scheduled promotions would result in discharge. If twenty years were not completed upon discharge, there was no retirement forthcoming. Twenty years also connoted that one had had a successful Navy career. It was the initial goal for most who entered military chaplaincy.

Our Navy service took us to San Diego, Quantico, Puerto Rico, Parris Island, and finally to Bethesda Naval Hospital. Promotions from JG to Lieutenant, and then Lieutenant Commander came on time, as expected. Upon arriving for duty at Bethesda, I had a total of fifteen years of active-duty service. Along the way, I received two Navy Commendation Medals, and was decorated for service with Marines on the ground in Desert Storm. No one expected that I would be passed over for promotion to Commander, but I was. I fell four years short of completing twenty. Pride made me angry. Pride made me embarrassed. Humility allowed me to stop the pity party and trust God.

I could blame my failure to promote on several factors: a chaplaincy that favors ministers of liturgical churches for promotion to higher grades, President Clinton and democrats who were down-sizing the military, minorities who are given some advantage in promotion in order to have a better mixture of races in the upper ranks, or that I wasn't creamy enough (cream always rises to the top). Except for the cream theme, every other explanation emerges from a prideful attempt to claim I deserved better. Even if I explain my failure to complete twenty years on the sovereign will of God, it is pride that feels a need to defend my dignity and worth. Humility doesn't require an explanation. Humility removes my own boot from my butt and straps it back to my foot where it belongs. There are mountains to climb, and I will need to wear both boots. After all, it's not about me. It is about blooming where you are planted, keeping your eyes fixed on Jesus, and walking by faith, not necessarily in that order.

Desert Storm

One of the chapters in my military career took place in 1991. Saddam Hussein of Iraq had moved his troops into Kuwait in August 1990, to occupy that tiny nation. George Bush Senior mobilized the U.S. military to force the Iraqi army out of Kuwait. A long buildup of our forces designated Operation Desert Shield was followed by the air and land battle called Operation Desert Storm. I was serving as the Marine Corp Recruit Training Regimental Chaplain at Parris Island, South Carolina when the build-up began. After our soldiers and Marines spent some long, hot months in Saudi Arabia, a few of our older chaplains suffered health problems. The senior Navy chaplain in charge of overseeing the command religious program for Marines in Saudi sent out a call for volunteers to replace chaplains who had to return to the states. I volunteered.

After a short orientation, which included training in the use of chemical weapons protective gear, the issuing of helmet, flak jacket, and other combat and desert gear, and a couple of weeks sitting around at Camp Lejeune, a 747 full of sailors, Marines and I were finally sent to Saudi. It was mid-January and Desert Storm was underway. Bombing raids were pounding the enemy on January 17th, just a few days before my arrival, and the same day that Iraq launched missiles at Israel. The enemy began launching the infamous scud missiles at U.S. troop locations. I was assigned to the 4th Marines as Regimental Chaplain. I had no previous desert training with Marines. In fact, my only experience with Marines was as the Family Service Center chaplain at Quantico, Virginia and as Regimental Chaplain at Parris Island. I now joined a unit already acclimated to the desert and sitting at combat readiness south of the Kuwait border.

Hussein's threat to use chemical weapons against our forces was on everyone's mind. About three weeks before G-day (February 24th) we donned our carbon-lined chemical over-suits and kept gas masks and MARK I antidote kits (atropine and pralidoxime) hanging on utility belts ready for use. All the U.S. military men and women had taken pretreatment tablets (pyridostigmine bromide), and many of us received a shot of an extremely painful concoction injected during preparation at Camp Lejeune. All of these measures suggested we were facing an eminent danger.

When death seems near and certain, more than fear of death occupies your gut. What will happen to my wife, children, and parents? What will they do? How will their future change? An internal battle caused several moments of panic during my first two weeks in the desert. Fear can completely immobilize, rendering you useless. Only when I was able to fully place my family in the hands of God and accept that my death was okay, did fear depart. I humbled myself to accept God's way, His will, and His decision to number my days. After that, my focus was no longer on me. It was on the men whom God had given me opportunity to counsel, encourage, and provide a spiritual perspective on the events which would follow.

I had so completely accepted that I would not survive Desert Storm, that returning home brought unexpected emotional confusion. What do I do now? There is more life to be lived. Death would have relieved me of any responsibility beyond the battle.

Since death failed to take me to Glory, I have to write the rest of the story. I humbly prayed, "Okay, God! Here we go! I'm yours."

Fat And Fifty

God gave me the best church in the whole world to serve as pastor. Connie, Rachel, Daniel, and I moved from my last Naval station Bethesda, Maryland, to a wonderful Baptist church southeast of Atlanta. Five years flew by, and my oldest child began planning her wedding. I think it was the day I sat in the bridal store watching Rachel try on wedding gowns that I began getting a lump in my throat. I was overweight, a few months from my 50th birthday, my son was a college freshman and my daughter was standing in front of me in a long, white, dress with a beautiful smile on her face. I was grumpy, and it was probably that day when I remember hearing Connie say, "Norman, it isn't about you."

Not many days later, I was still swallowing hard, hoping I could lead my daughter and her groom through the wedding ceremony without losing it. I walked her down the aisle, joined her hand to his, and stepped up on the platform to take my place as minister. It was May 15th. My 50th birthday was in nine days! My daughter is getting married! Inside I was screaming, "Ahhh-hhhhhhhh!!!"

Life doesn't ever stand still. It keeps moving faster and faster and faster. I find that I must periodically slap myself, then move self out of the way and celebrate the lives of people around me. Humility is about enjoying people. Self-centered and selfish living is life with both eyes shut. Look! This bride and this groom are in love and beginning a home where God is at the center. Their joy on this day is a wonderful thing. It isn't about me. It is about this special moment in the life of my little girl. "Bless her, dear Lord. Bless her husband with strength and wisdom. Bless the two of them with enduring love for You and for each other. And, may they provide me lots of grandchildren. Amen. Oops! Forgive the grandchildren wish, Lord. I know it is not about me."

Alternative Ministry

I was pastor of a sweet Alabama church for two years. Then I was Navy chaplain for thirteen years. Then I was pastor in Georgia for nine years. Every minister will tell you that God led them in each new direction of their ministry. I believe God now directed my life to move from pastor to become chaplain at a rescue mission. It was a great ministry for 15 months. Then I was presented with a difficult decision. Could I, after being in the top spiritual leadership position as a chaplain or pastor for a total of 25 years, accept a job to be an assistant? Here is the kicker: My brother-in-law had served as pastor of a wonderful church for thirty years. Was I humble enough to be his associate and fully accept his leadership over me? Was I humble enough to endure the perception others would have of me? Will the word *nepotism* unnerve me? Will pride force me to constantly defend my worthiness beyond my relation to the pastor's wife? I sniffed the air and believed God was leading me there.

Pride can cause us to miss great blessings from God. If all our decisions are made from a "what about me" consideration, our big "I" will completely obscure the road signs along our journey. We miss important turns and end up down roads God never intended us to take. There were many positive signs before and after my decision to accept my Bro-in-law's offer. He unselfishly shared his ministry and graciously treated me as partner. God has blessed me with opportunity to grow in new directions. My writing ministry has been another blessing from God and an affirmation of His continued work in me. God is good!

Humility holds us in place and gives our lives stability. You know what I mean. Pride makes us gaze at the grass on the other side of the fence. Pride makes us quit when someone questions our authority. Selfishness runs away when there is too much required of us. Self-preservation leads us to withdraw from the fight. Pride keeps record of offenses and sets a limit for how much it will take. Self-centeredness draws a line in the sand and dares anyone to step over it. Humility doesn't keep score, doesn't give up, and doesn't run away. It is all about trusting the Lord, loving others, and living in obedience to God's Word. It's about Him.

I suspect that anyone who remains as pastor at one church for over thirty years is probably familiar with humility. I also believe that pride is part of the cause for the statistic that the average length of time pastors stay at a church is less than 5 years. They bounce from church to church either because they run out of sermons, or they are tempted to accept the invitation of a larger church, or they grow tired of the battle and need a fresh group of Christians to do battle with, or they believe they have accomplished all that their skills and gifts can accomplish where they have been serving. I think pride is hidden in all those reasons somewhere. Maybe pride is at the root of my imagining that I am able to judge those pastors who do not stay long years at any church. I thank God for allowing me to spend nine years of ministry serving alongside my brother-in-law and sister.

Fighting Old Age

I didn't take 50 well, and turning 60 is no picnic either. There are a lot of bad things that happen as we grow older. If one's health is good at 60, one can be certain that it won't last long. I have always been dismayed by those senior citizens who felt they had to take hands-full of pills each day. I now know how quickly pills are compounded by one condition after another. As the pill count goes up, our number of functioning body parts goes down. Our number of daily life decisions also decreases. Other people start making those decisions for us. I have watched this whole process in the lives of old people more closely than I did ten years ago. Old people become consulted less, needed less, and listened to less. Those who are younger gradually dominate the entire universe around us. Soon, all of the doctors, lawyers, teachers, police officers, and preachers are younger than our own children. The professional people we know retire and then pass away. Friends and relatives pass from our lives one by one.

It is easy to become more self-centered than ever as we become old. In the past we may have won the struggle to keep our focus on God and others. Age seems to me to be the most vicious opponent of all. How can we hurt all over, continually lose control of choices, watch younger people dominate every area of our lives, increase in awareness of things we can no longer do, grieve over an annual list of lost loved ones, and still be able to say, "It's not about me?"

There are some old people I have known who wore humility with such confidence and grace that I was in awe of them. I measure other old people by them. I want to believe that humility is a choice. We can choose to moan and groan about our suffering. We can constantly reminisce about the things that were.

We can stew over all the things *they* are doing to me and my world. We can make every conversation be about me, my, and mine. Older people whom I have watched do these things seem to find joy only when they can make other people as miserable as they are. I realize that saying that doesn't make me look very merciful or compassionate. My hope is that I will reject that picture and choose a different avocation for my ancient years. Hold that thought.

With the beginning of a new year in which I would soon celebrate my 65th birthday, we were also approaching my Bro-in-law's retirement. When a Baptist church installs a new pastor, he should be able to fill ministry positions with his own staff. I fully accepted that. I have gone through many transitions in ministry but never at my current age. I had been seeking a new pastoral position for more than a year as I anticipated the need to allow the new pastor to choose his own associate. There were no offers. There were many prayers but no answers. I considered that God may be choosing to retire me.

Four months before the pastoral change would take place, the co-pastor who had been tapped to assume command very graciously asked if I would be interested in serving as chaplain for the church's assisted living community. Wow! What was God doing to me? This had not been something on my radar. I was very aware of this ministry but had no thoughts of it. Within minutes of his asking, God sent a flood of thoughts and feelings through my heart and mind that surprised me and excited me. He was answering my prayer very differently than I ever expected.

All those thoughts I was having about my own aging became a means of identifying with and loving my new opportunities for ministering. God allowed me over the next six years to serve Him and this elder community while learning more about my own humility and the humility required in this phase of life.

Not The End

Every phase of life, from beginning to end, is best when handled humbly. Placing God and others above self, rejecting a prideful attitude, and placing service and love far above power, prestige, or personal welfare will yield a life of precious memories and fewer regrets. Perhaps, only at the end of life will hindsight reveal to us the magnitude of the fulfillment of God's promise to us for being humble before Him. *"Humble yourselves, therefore, under the mighty hand of God, that He may exalt you at the proper time"* (Proverbs 15:6; Luke 14:11; Luke 18:14; James 4:10; 1 Peter 5:6).

We could say that having lived a humble life, upon reaching our latter years, our "proper time" has probably already come and gone. We were humble. God exalted us. Then we retire. A time must come when our "proper time" has finished its course. The senior pastor becomes a church member. The Master Sergeant becomes a Walmart greeter. The Air Traffic Control person gets a hotdog cart in the city park. The business executive spends her days writing haiku for greeting cards. The President of the United States gets his greatest pleasure parachuting tandem.

If that all sounds pessimistic, it isn't my intention. It is meant to reiterate the high value of humility. If we live for self and selfish purposes, the phases of our lives will provide multiple opportunities for bitterness, anger, resentment, and dissatisfaction. When our desire is to be humble as we face each new direction in life, we will find multiple opportunities for unselfish service. True humility will always be a source of joy, pleasure and contentment no matter what our position, condition, or age. In fact, humility teaches us that when we are humble before our God, opportunities to be selfless and serve are never over until the end. May one of our greatest desires always be humility until the end. And, this is not the end.

ABOUT THE AUTHOR

The author's 45 years in full-time Christian ministry has encompassed a wide-range of experiences, including five years in youth ministry, eleven years as pastor, a short 15-month chaplaincy with a rescue mission, thirteen years as Navy Chaplain, nine years as the associate pastor of a large church with multi-ministries, and six years as chaplain at one of those ministries.

Norman has dabbled in writing for most of his life but only became serious about it in 2003 when he felt compelled to write a book to address the position Southern Baptists took against allowing women as senior pastors. *Women Pastors* is published by Tate Publishing in Mustang, Oklahoma and is now out of print.

In 2012 Norman published an ebook with WestBowPress titled *True Humility*. That book has now been revised and published with the same title. After years of work on another book, in 2021 Norman published *The Commandments of Jesus* with WestBowPress. This book takes the words of Jesus "Teaching them to observe all things that I have commanded you..." (Matthew 28:20) and addresses the question, What commands?

Connie, Norman's sweet wife, has been by his side for 47 years. She retired in 2021 from her job as the school nurse at an elementary school in Fort Benning, GA. Their daughter, Rachel, is mother to their six grandchildren. She is a graduate of Georgia State University and a pastor's wife. Their son, Daniel, is a graduate of the University of Georgia and an IT specialist and mobile applications director at Southern Regional Extension, Forestry.

BIBLIOGRAPHY

Bachelder, Louise, ed. *Abraham Lincoln, Wisdom & Wit*. Mount Vernon, New York: The Peter Pauper Press, 1965.

Bennett, William J., ed., *The Book of Virtues*. New York: Simon & Schuster, 1993.

Bennett, William J., ed. *The Moral Compass*. New York: Simon & Schuster, 1995.

Cobb, Nancy and Connie Grigsby. *How To Get Your Husband To Talk To You*. Sisters, OR: Multnomah Publishers, Inc., 2001.

Edman, V Raymond. *The Disciplines of Life*. Minneapolis: World Wide Publications, 1948.

Ephron, Nora. *Heartburn*. New York: Vintage Books, 1996.

Funk, Charles Earle. *Hog On Ice & Other Curious Expressions*. New York, NY: Harper & Row, Publishers, 1985.

Gray, Alice, comp. *Stories for the Heart*. Sisters, Oregon: Multnomah Books, 1996.

Hester, Dennis J., comp., *The Vance Havner Quote Book*. Grand Rapids: Baker Book House, 1986.

Hutchins, Robert Maynard. ed., *Great Books of The Western World*. Chicago: Encyclopaedia Britannica, Inc., 1986. vol. 22, *Chaucer*, by Geoffrey Chaucer.

Kardong, Terrence G. *Benedict's Rule, A Translation and Commentary*. Collegeville, Minn: The Liturgical Press, 1996.

Lewis, C.S. *The Screwtape Letters*. 1961 ed., First Touchstone Edition. New York: Touchstone, 1996.

Macarthur, John F., *The Pillars of Christian Character*. Wheaton: Crossway Books, 1998.

Mahaney, C.J., *Humility: True Greatness*. Colorado Springs: Multnomah Books, 2005.

Maxwell, John C., *Be A People Person*. Colorado Springs: Chariot Victor Publishing, 1994.

Morgan, Robert J., *Nelson's Complete Book of Stories, Illustrations, & Quotes*. Nashville: Thomas Nelson, Inc., 2000.

Murray, Andrew, *Humility*. Gainesville, FL: Bridge-Logos, 2000.

Poor Richard's Almanac. Mount Vernon, NY: Peter Pauper Press, 1983.

Reimann, James, ed. *My Utmost for His Highest: An Updated Edition In Today's Language*, Oswald Chambers. Michigan: Discovery House Publishers, 1992.

Segalove, Ilene and Paul Bob Velick. *List Your Self:Listmaking as the Way to Self-Discovery*. Kansas City: Andrews and McMeel, 1996.

Selden, John, *Table Talk: Being the Discourses of John Selden, Esq. . . Relating Especially to Religion and State*, 1689.

The Joyful Christian, 127 Readings From C.S.Lewis. New York: Macmillan Publishing Co., Inc., 1977.

Wagner, C. Peter, *Humility.* Ventura, California: Regal Books, 2002.

White, E.B., *Charlotte's Web.* Harper Collins, 1952.

www.ingramcontent.com/pod-product-compliance
Lightning Source LLC
Chambersburg PA
CBHW060316050426
42449CB00011B/2512